W9-BDD-676

Know It, Show It

GRADE 1

Printed in the U.S.A.

ISBN 978-1-328-45320-4

2 3 4 5 6 7 8 9 10   0982   27 26 25 24 23 22 21 20 19

4500750068   B C D E F G

Grade
1

Contents

Name _____

Words to Know

Learn these words. You will see them in your reading and use them in your writing.

Word Bank

go	is	like	see
the	this	to	we

▶ Write the word that best completes each sentence.

1. We _____*go*_____ to  .

2. We _____*see*_____ this  .

3. We sat at ___*the*___  .

4. We go ___*to*___ the  .

▶ Write a sentence for a word you did not write yet.

_____

_____

Name _____

Short *a*

You can spell the **short a** sound with **a**, as in **mat**.

▶ Write each Spelling Word in the correct column.

**Words with short
a at the beginning**

am

at

**Words with short
a in the middle**

mat

sat

bat

sam

Spelling Words
Basic
mat
sat
bat
Sam
am
at

Name _____

Consonants *m*, *s*, *t*, *b*; Short *a*

▶ Say each picture name. Write the consonant for the beginning sound in each word.

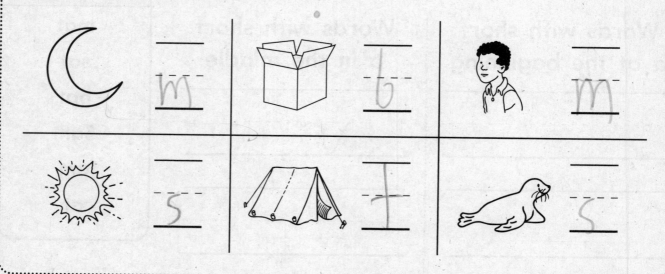

m _____   b _____   m _____

s _____   t _____   s _____

The word **sat** has the **short a** vowel sound. The letter **a** stands for that sound.

▶ If a picture name has the **short a** sound, write **a**. (One word does **not** have **short a**, so leave it blank!)

m_a_t   b___t   b_a_t

Name _____

Short *a*

You can spell the **short a** sound with **a**, as in **mat**.

▶ Write the Spelling Word that names each picture.

1.

Sam

2.

mat

3.

bat

4.

sat

▶ Which two Spelling Words did you **not** use? Circle them in the list. Then write a word that rhymes with each one.

Name _____

Phonics Review

When a word has one **vowel** followed by a **consonant**, the vowel sound is usually short. The letter **a** in the word **am** stands for the **short a** sound.

▶ Write words to rhyme with **am** and **at**. For each word's first letter, choose among **m, s, S, T, t,** and **b**.

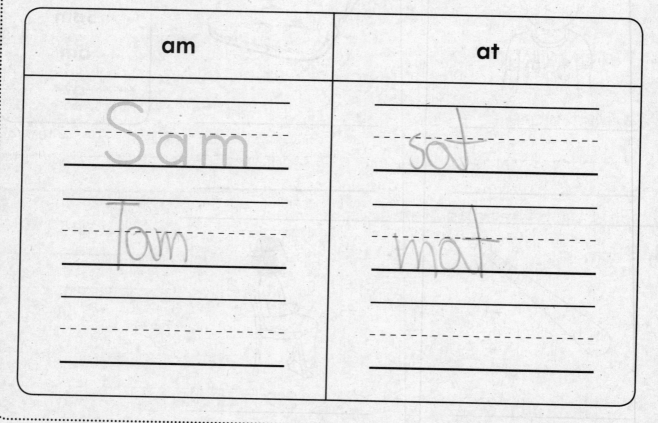

am	at
Sam	sat
Tam	mat

▶ Use a word you wrote to complete the sentence.

Sam is at _____ .

Name _____

Power Words: Match

┌─────────────── Word Bank ───────────────┐

try   new   great   enjoy   excited   nervous

└──┘

▶ Write the Power Word from **Try This!** that best fits each item.

1. Which word means **not old**?

new

2. Which word tells that you really like doing something?

try

3. This word means **better than good**.

great

4. Which word tells how you might feel when you try something new?

nevous

5. You feel this way when you are very happy.

excited

6. This word tells what you do when you work hard.

enjoy

Name _____

Words About Feelings

Adjectives are words that describe people, places, or things.
Words about feelings describe how a person feels.

▶ Read each word that describes a feeling. If you do not
know the meaning of a word, look it up in the dictionary.
Write the word below the picture that shows that feeling.

Feeling Words

happy	mad	calm	sad

1. _happy_

2. _sad_

3. _calm_

4. _mad_

Name _____

Author's Purpose

The reason an author writes is called the **author's purpose**. An author can write to **persuade**, **inform**, or **entertain**. To figure out an author's purpose, start by looking for clues about the **genre**. Then ask questions about what you read.

▶ Answer the questions about **Try This!**

🔍 Pages 20–21 What does this text tell about? Why does the author tell about these new things?

_____

- -

_____

- -

_____

🔍 Page 24 Why did the author write this text? What does the author want you to learn?

_____

- -

_____

- -

_____

Name _____

Classify and Categorize

To **classify** words, sort the words into a group.
To **categorize** words, name the group of words
or tell how the words are alike.

▶ Read the name of each category. Then write words
from the word bank under the correct category.

Word Bank

ride	park	sing	bank
store	zoo	dance	sleep

Places	Actions
stor	ride
zoo	sing
park	dance
bank	sleep

Name _____

Collaborative Conversations

Collaborative conversations happen when you talk about something with teachers or other children at school. Remember these rules:

- Decide if you should use **formal** or **informal language**.
- Speak loudly and clearly.
- Take turns talking and use complete sentences.
- Listen carefully and respond to what others say.
- Ask questions when you don't understand something.

▶ Follow the rules above as you discuss the following questions about **Try This!** with a partner. Then mark each rule that you followed during your conversation.

1. Look at pages 16–17. What do you think is the best way to get to school? Why?

_____

- -

_____

2. What games are the children on pages 22–23 playing? Which game do you like best? Why?

_____

- -

_____

Name _____

3. What are children learning to do on page 24? Which one do you think is the hardest thing to learn? Why?

_____

- - - - - - - - - - - - - - - - - - -

_____

- - - - - - - - - - - - - - - - - - -

_____

- - - - - - - - - - - - - - - - - - -

_____

4. Which rules did you follow in your conversation?

☐ Use formal language.

☐ Use informal language.

☐ Speak loudly and clearly.

☐ Take turns.

☐ Use complete sentences.

☐ Listen carefully.

☐ Respond to what other people say.

☐ Ask questions.

Name _____

Words to Know

a	first	good	had
he	I	my	was

▶ Write a word from the box to complete each sentence.

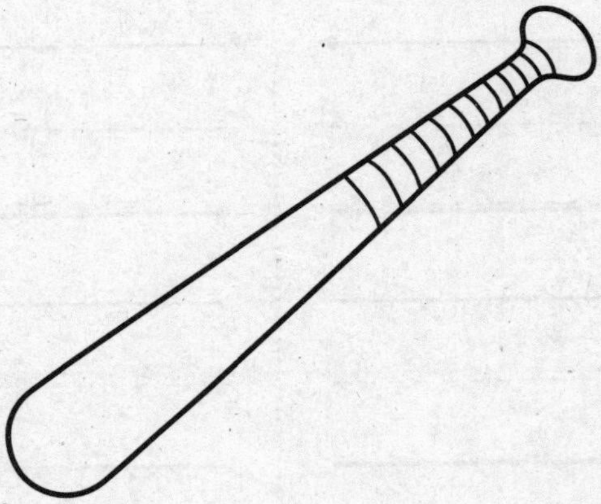

1. Cam ____had____ a bat.

2. ____he____ can bat.

3. I am ____good____ !

4. I like ____my____ bat!

▶ Write sentences using two new words from the box.

_____

_____

_____

15

Name _____

Short *a*

You can spell the **short a** sound with **a**, as in **cat**.

▶ Write each Basic and Review Spelling Word in the correct column.

Words with *an*	Words with *at*	Other words
an	cat	bad
can	at	nap
pan	sat	an
	bat	

Spelling Words

Basic

an
bad
can
nap
cat
pan

Review

am
at
sat
bat

Name _____

Consonants *n*, *d*, *p*, *c*; Short *a*

▶ Say each picture name. Write the consonant for the beginning sound in each word.

| | d | | c | | p |

| | n | | m | | c |

The word **cat** has the **short a** vowel sound. The letter **a** stands for that sound.

▶ If a picture name has the **short a** sound, write **a**. (Two words do **not** have **short a**, so leave them blank!)

c __a__ n   b __a__ t   s __ __ n

p __a__ d   c __ __ p   c __a__ p

Name _____

Short *a*

You can spell the **short a** sound with **a**, as in **can**.

▶ Say the name of each picture. Write the Basic and Review Spelling Words that rhyme with the picture name.

Spelling Words

Basic

an

bad

can

nap

cat

pan

Review

am

at

sat

bat

1.   bad   sad

2.   nap   cap

3.  pan   can

   an   fan

4.   cat   hat

   at   sat

▶ Which Review Spelling Word did you **not** use? Say a sentence that uses the word.

Name _____

Power Words: Draw and Write

(Word Bank)

trip	partner	wished	last

▶ Draw a picture or write words that will help you remember each Power Word from **My School Trip**. Try to write more than you draw.

1. trip	2. partner

3. wished	**4. last**

Name _____

Author's Purpose

The reason an author writes is called the **author's purpose**.
An author can write to **persuade**, **inform**, or **entertain**. To
figure out an author's purpose, look for clues to the **genre**.
Then ask questions about what you read.

▶ Answer the questions about **My School Trip.**

🔍 Pages 38–39 What kind of text is this? How do you know?

_____
- -
_____
_____
- -
_____

🔍 Page 42 Why do you think the author wrote this story?
What do you think the author wants you to learn?

_____
- -
_____
_____
- -
_____
_____
- -
_____

Name _____

Phonics Review

The **a** in **pat** stands for the **short a** sound. The **a** is closed in, or followed by, the consonant **t**. When a word has only one vowel followed by a consonant, the vowel sound is usually short.

▶ Write each picture name below.

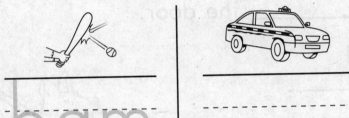

bam

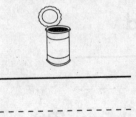

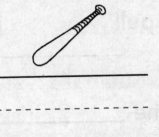

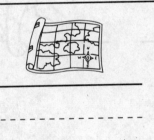

▶ Write a sentence using one of the words you wrote.

_____

_____

_____

_____

Inflection *–ed*

A **verb** is an action word. The **ending –ed** can be added to a verb to tell that the action happened in the past.

▶ Choose the word that best completes each sentence. Write the word on the line.

1. Dad will _____lock_____ the door.

   lock   **locked**

2. Spot _____pulled_____ on the leash.

   pull   **pulled**

3. She _____helped_____ me.

   help   **helped**

4. We will _____mix_____ the soup.

   mix   **mixed**

5. Dad _____rested_____ in the chair.

   rest   **rested**

Name _____

Power Words: Yes or No?

▶ Read each sentence. Circle **YES** if the word makes sense or **NO** if it does not. Rewrite the sentence so it makes sense.

Word Bank

together

kinds

1. One person can work **together**.

YES   NO

Two persons con work together.

2. Maps are **kinds** of pets.

YES   NO

Dogs are kinds of pets.

Name _____

Central Idea

The **topic** of an informational text is the person or thing a text is about. The **central idea** is the most important point about the topic.

▶ Answer the questions about **A Kids' Guide to Friends.**

🔍 Pages 52–53 What is this part of the text about? What evidence helps you understand this?

_____

- -

_____

_____

- -

_____

🔍 Pages 58–60 What does the author want you to understand from reading this text? Which details help you figure out the central idea?

_____

- -

_____

_____

- -

_____

Name _____

Words to Know

Word Bank

and	find	for	just
many	one	she	then

▶ Write a word from the box to complete each sentence.

1. I had _____one_____ cat.

2. My cat is _____just_____ one good cat!

3. My cat can _____find_____ a mat.

4. _____she_____ likes to nap.

5. _____then_____ she taps my cap.

6. I will hug _____and_____ pat her.

▶ Think of a sentence for one of the words you did not write. Tell it to a partner.

Name _____

Short *i*

You can spell the **short i** sound with **i**, as in **pin**.

▶ Write each Basic and Review Spelling Word in the correct column.

Words with short *i*	Words with short *a*
it	pan
him	an
iis	nap
sip	cat
fit	
pin	

Spelling Words

Basic

it
him
is
sip
fit
pin

Review

pan
an
nap
cat

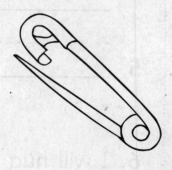

Name _____

Consonants *r, f, s /z/;* Short *i*

> ▶ Say each picture name. Write the consonant for the beginning sound in each word.

r   r   f

r   f   f

The word **rip** has the **short i** vowel sound. The letter **i** stands for that sound.

Word Bank

dip

is

fin

> ▶ Write the word from the box to complete each sentence.

1. This __is__ Tim.

2. Tim can __dip__ in.

3. We see just one __fin__ , Tim!

Name _____

Short *i*

You can spell the **short i** sound with **i**, as in **rip**.

▶ Write the missing letter to complete each Basic Spelling Word. Then write the word.

1. h __i__ m   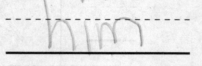 him

2. s __i__ p    sip

3. __i__ t   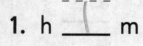 it

4. p __i__ n   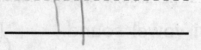 pin

5. f __i__ t   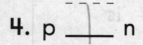 fit

6. __i__ s    is

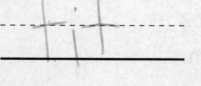

Spelling Words
Basic
it
him
is
sip
fit
pin
Review
pan
an
nap
cat

Name _____

Power Words: Match

| Word Bank |
| ugly   beautiful   paddled   chilly   changed |

▶ Write the Power Word from **Big Dilly's Tale** that best fits each item.

1. Which word would you use to tell about a very pretty picture? 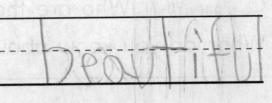 beautiful

2. This word means **to become different**. 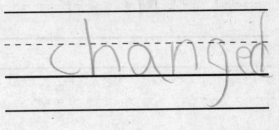 changed

3. Which word means **not good-looking**? ugly

4. This word tells how something moved through water. 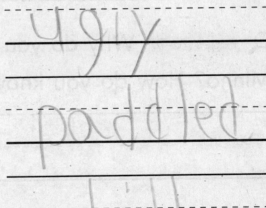 paddled

5. Which word means almost the same as **cold**? 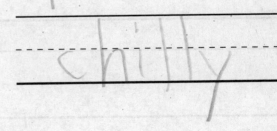 chilly

Name _____

Characters

A **character** is the person, animal, or thing a story is about. Understanding what a character is like can help you understand and describe the **reasons** for their **actions**.

▶ Answer the questions about **Big Dilly's Tale.**

🔍 Pages 70–71 Who are the characters in the story? What do you know about them?

_____

- -

_____

_____

- -

_____

🔍 Pages 76–77 Why do you think Dilly went to find Minna? How do you know?

_____

- -

_____

_____

- -

_____

_____

- -

_____

Name _____

Phonics Review

- A **vowel** followed by one consonant usually stands for the short vowel sound. The word **fin** has the **short i** sound.
- You can add the **–s** ending to change a word. The word **fins** means more than one **fin**.

▶ Say each picture name. Write the word that names the picture.

fan fans	fin fins
fans	fins
rip rips	can cans
rips	can
bin bins	pin pins
bin	pins
bat bats	pad pads
bats	pad

Name _____

Inflection –ed

A **verb** is an action word. The **ending –ed** can be added
to a verb to tell that the action happened in the past.

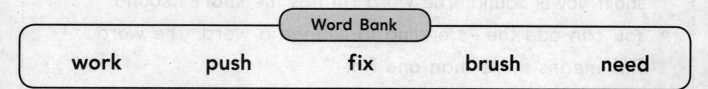

Word Bank

work   push   fix   brush   need

▶ Choose the word that best completes each sentence.
Add **–ed** if the verb needs to tell about the past.
Write the word on the line.

1. I ___work___ on a puzzle yesterday.

2. I ___brush___ the cat now.

3. Yesterday, I ___fix___ my sister's stroller.

4. Mom ___push___ the chair last week.

5. I ___need___ crayons to color.

Grade 1

32

Module 1 • Week 3

Name _____

Words to Know

Knowing how to read and write these words can make you a better reader and writer.

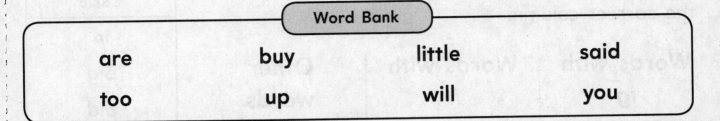

Word Bank

are	buy	little	said
too	up	will	you

▶ Write a word from the box to complete each sentence.

1. Sam and Dan ___are___ kids.

2. Sam and Dan see a ___little___ cat.

3. Dan will ___buy___ a mat for it.

4. The little cat ___will___ nap.

▶ Write a sentence for a word you did not write yet.

_____

_____

_____

Name _____

Short *i*

You can spell the **short i** sound with **i**, as in **sit**.

▶ Write each Basic and Review Spelling Word in the correct column.

Words with *ig*	Words with *it*	Other words
pig	sit	did
dig	fit	in
big	it	pig

Spelling Words

Basic

in

pig

did

sit

dig

big

Review

pin

fit

it

sip

Name _____

Consonants *g, k*

The letter **g** is a consonant. The word **gab** begins with the letter and sound for **g**. The letter **k** is a consonant. The word **kit** begins with the letter and sound for **k**.

▶ Name each picture. Write the consonant for the beginning sound.

g	k	k
g	k	g

▶ Write a word to complete each sentence.

1. This is ___Kid___ .

2. Kid can get a ___fig___ .

3. Kid can put it in the ___bag___ .

Name _____

Short *i*

You can spell the **short i** sound with **i**, as in **dig**.

▶ Say the name of each picture. Write the Basic and Review Spelling Words that rhyme with it.

1.    _____   _____

2.    _____   _____

3.   pig   big

     dig

4.   fit   it

     sit

▶ Which Review Spelling Word did you **not** use? Circle it in the list. Then say a sentence that uses the word.

Name _____

Phonics Review

When a word has one vowel that is followed by a consonant, the vowel usually has a short vowel sound. The **a** in **gas** stands for the **short a** sound. The **i** in **kid** stands for the **short i** sound.

▶ Write the word that names each picture. The first one is done for you.

fit (fig)

fig

wig   wag

wig

kin (kit)

kit

bag   big

bag

(gas)   gab

gas

(kid)   did

kid

▶ Write a sentence using one of the words you wrote.

_____

_____

Name _____

Power Words: Match

```
┌─────────────────────( Word Bank )─────────────────────┐
│                                                         │
│    market              help              neighbors      │
│                                                         │
│    sell                mess              set            │
│                                                         │
└─────────────────────────────────────────────────────────┘
```

▶ Write the Power Word from **Dan Had a Plan**
that best fits each item.

1. These people live near
   each other.

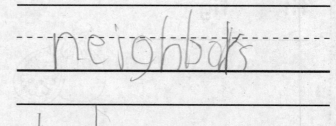

2. What can you do for
   a friend?

3. This word means to get
   money for something.

4. This word is something
   that is not neat.

5. What is a place to
   buy things?

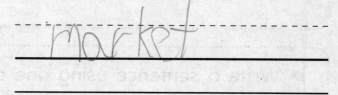

6. This word means to make
   something easy to use.

38

Name _____

Words About Places and Things

A **noun** that names a **place** tells where something is happening.
A **noun** that names a **thing** tells what something is.

▶ Write a word from the box to finish each sentence. Draw
a circle to tell if the word names a **place** or a **thing**. Find
words you do not know in a dictionary.

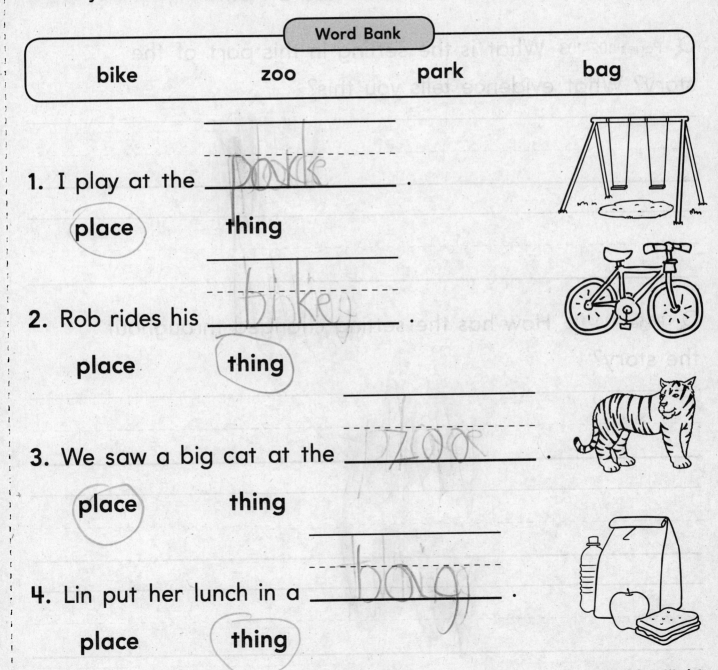

Word Bank

| bike | zoo | park | bag |

1. I play at the ___park___ .

   (place)   thing

2. Rob rides his ___bike___ .

   place   (thing)

3. We saw a big cat at the ___zoo___ .

   (place)   thing

4. Lin put her lunch in a ___bag___ .

   place   (thing)

Name _____

Setting

The **setting** is where and when the story takes place. Readers can use **details** in the words and pictures to **describe** the setting. The setting can be a place, time of day, or time of year.

▶ Answer the questions about **Dan Had a Plan**.

🔍 Pages 102–103 What is the setting in this part of the story? What evidence tells you this?

_____
- -
_____
- -
_____
- -
_____

🔍 Pages 110–112 How has the setting changed throughout the story?

_____
- -
_____
- -
_____
- -
_____

Name _____

Antonyms

An **antonym** is a word that has the opposite meaning of another word.

▶ Read each sentence. Choose the word from the box that means the opposite of the underlined word. Write it on the line.

> **Word Bank**
>
> happy   slow   huge   before

1. Tam ate a cookie <u>after</u> dinner.

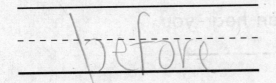

2. A dog runs <u>fast</u>.

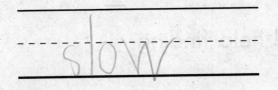

3. The <u>tiny</u> bug is hard to see.

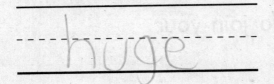

4. The baby is <u>sad</u>.

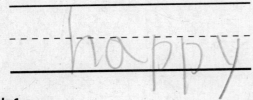

Name _____

Social Communication

Remember these rules when you talk to others:

- Decide if you should use **formal language** or **informal language.**

- Be polite.

- Tell your name to new people.

- Share something about yourself.

- Tell what you need or feel.

- Listen carefully and look at the speaker.

- Speak loudly and clearly so others can hear you.

- Draw to help explain your ideas.

▶ Follow the rules to act out talking about these topics with a partner. Then mark the rules you followed.

1. You are new in school and need help finding your classroom.

2. You are trying to get someone to join your soccer team.

Name _____

3. You are telling a cousin why your town is so great.

4. Which rules did you follow?

_____

- - - - - - - - - - - - - - - - - - -

_____

- - - - - - - - - - - - - - - - - - -

_____

☐ Use formal language.

☐ Use informal language.

☐ Be polite.

☐ Tell your name.

☐ Share something about yourself.

☐ Tell what you need or what you are feeling.

☐ Listen carefully.

☐ Look at the speaker.

☐ Speak loudly and clearly.

☐ Draw ideas to help explain.

☐ Use complete sentences.

Name _____

Words to Know

Word Bank

do   live   of   our

wants   what   with   your

▶ Circle the word that best completes each sentence.

1. This is (our, do) dad.

2. He (wants, what) a map.

3. I go (of, with) him.

4. (Our, What) is this?

5. (Do, Live) you see a map?

6. (Your, With) map is big!

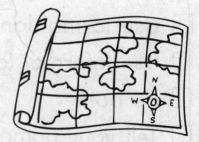

▶ Write a sentence for a word you did not use yet.

_____

_ _ _ _ _ _ _ _ _ _ _ _ _ _ _ _ _ _

_____

_ _ _ _ _ _ _ _ _ _ _ _ _ _ _ _ _ _

_____

Name _____

Short o

You can spell the **short o** sound with **o**, as in **log**.

▶ Write each Basic and Review Spelling Word in the correct column.

Spelling Words
Basic
log
not
top
hot
hop
on
Review
big
sit
pig
dig

Words with short o	Words with short i
log	big
not	sit
top	pig
hot	dig
on	
hop	

Name _____

Consonants *l*, *h*; Short *o*

When a word has one **vowel** that is followed by a **consonant**, the vowel usually has a short vowel sound. The word **lot** has a **short o** sound. It begins with consonant **l**. The word **hot** has a **short o** sound. It begins with consonant **h**.

▶ Name each picture. Write the letter that stands for the missing sound.

l og	d o g	h op
l id	p o t	l ap
m o p	t o p	h at

Name _____

Short o

You can spell the **short o** sound with **o**, as in **hop**.

▶ Write the missing letter. Then write the Basic Spelling Word on the line.

Basic

log
not
top
hot
hop
on

Review

big
sit
pig
dig

1. h_o_p 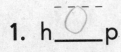 hop

2. l_o_g 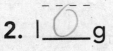 log

3. _o_n on

4. n_o_t 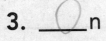 not

5. h_o_t 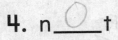 hot

6. t_o_p 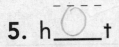 top

Name _____

Power Words: Yes or No?

▶ Read each sentence. Circle **YES** if the word makes sense or **NO** if it does not. Rewrite the sentence so it makes sense.

1. People cannot live in a **town**.

 YES   NO

People can liv in a town.

2. I can find a sock on a **map**.

YES   NO

I can fin a school on a map.

Name _____

Text Features

Authors of informational texts use text features to explain ideas and help readers find information. **Bold text** helps readers notice important words. A **label** tells what a picture is. A **map** is a small picture of a big place. A **symbol** is a small picture that stands for something else.

▶ Answer the questions about **On the Map!**

🔍 Page 123 What do the map and symbols show? Why do you think the author included them?

they compare a map

to a photo

🔍 Page 126 Why does the author include the photos and labels on this page? How do the labels help you?

_____

_____

_____

_____

Phonics Review

One **vowel** followed by a **consonant** usually has a short vowel sound. The word **hat** has a **short a** sound. The word **hit** has a **short i** sound. The word **hot** has a **short o** sound.

▶ Choose and write two words to complete each sentence.

1. Kim __has__ a big __hat__ .

    hot   **hat**   **has**   **his**

2. The __dog__ sits in my __lap__ .

    cat   **dog**   **lap**   **lip**

3. This __pot__ is __hot__ .

    pot   **not**   **hot**   **lot**

4. We __got__ in the __cab__ .

    cot   **cab**   **gas**   **got**

5. I can __hit__ with the __bat__ .

    lit   **bat**   **hit**   **lot**

Name _____

Words About Places and Things

Nouns that name a **place** tell where something is happening.
Nouns that name a **thing** tell what something is.

▶ Write a word from the box to finish each sentence. Draw a
circle to tell if the word names a **place** or a **thing**. Find any
words you do not know in a dictionary.

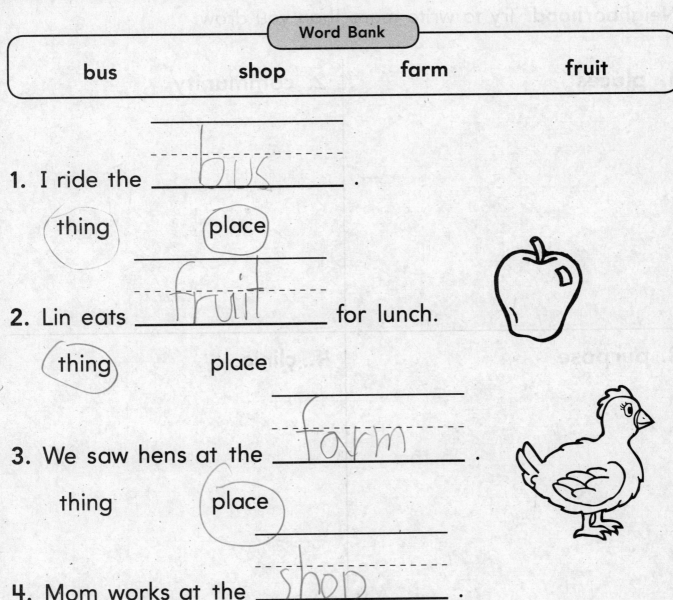

Word Bank
bus   shop   farm   fruit

1. I ride the ___bus___ .

  (thing)   (place)

2. Lin eats ___fruit___ for lunch.

  (thing)   place

3. We saw hens at the ___farm___ .

  thing   (place)

4. Mom works at the ___shop___ .

  thing   (place)

Name _____

Power Words: Draw and Write

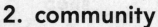

Word Bank

| places | community | purpose | clinic |

▶ Draw a picture or write words that will help you remember each Power Word from **Places in My Neighborhood**. Try to write more than you draw.

1. places	2. community
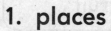	

3. purpose	4. clinic

Name _____

Content-Area Words

Some informational texts have science or social studies words. If you don't know their meaning, you can ask yourself questions about them. Then you can use **context clues** to figure out their meanings.

▶ Answer the questions about **Places in My Neighborhood**.

🔍 Pages 137–138 How can the heading and photo help you figure out the meaning of **city**?

_____

- -

_____

- -

_____

🔍 Page 140 What questions could help you figure out the meaning of **officer**? How could you answer them?

_____

- -

_____

- -

_____

- -

_____

Name _____

Words to Know

▶ Write the word from the box that best completes each sentence.

1. _____Who_____ wants to eat?

2. Tom wants to _____eat_____ .

3. We will _____make_____ it in a pot.

4. _____Put_____ the pot here.

5. Tip it _____out_____ of the tin.

6. Tom is _____ to eat.

7. He _____takes_____ a sip.

8. _____Who_____ is it, Tom?

Word Bank

about

eat

How

make

out

Put

takes

Who

Name _____

Short *u*

You can spell the **short u** sound with **u**, as in **nut**.

▶ Write each Basic and Review Spelling Word in the correct column.

Words with short *u*	Words with short *o*
up	log
bug	hop
mud	hot
nut	not
hug	
tub	

Spelling Words

Basic

up

bug

mud

nut

hug

tub

Review

log

hop

hot

not

Name _____

Consonants *w*, *j*, *y*, *v*; Short *u*

The letters **w**, **j**, **y**, and **v** are consonants.

▶ Name each picture. Write the consonant for the beginning sound.

When a word has one **vowel** that is followed by a **consonant**, the vowel usually has a short sound. The word **yum** has a **short u** sound.

▶ Write the word that names the picture.

Name _____

Short *u*

You can spell the **short u** sound with **u**, as in **tub**.

▶ Write the Basic Spelling Word that names each picture.

1.

   bug

2.

   up

3.

   hug

4.

   mud

5.

   nut

6.

   tub

57

Name _____

Power Words: Match

Word Bank		
spoon	against	churn
stock	heal	drive

▶ Write the Power Word from **Who Put the Cookies in the Cookie Jar?** that best fits each item.

1. Which word tells how to help someone get well?

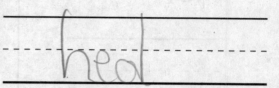

2. Which word tells a way to pick up food?

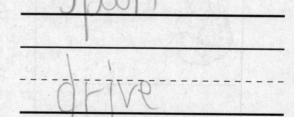

3. This word tells how to make a car move.

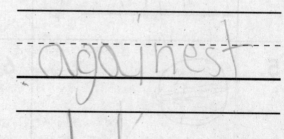

4. Which word tells about keeping something from being hurt?

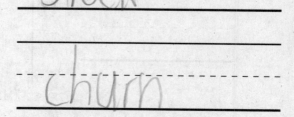

5. Which word tells how you fill up a shelf?

6. This word means almost the same as **stir**.

Name _____

Text Organization

Authors choose a **text organization**, or way to arrange information, that fits their reason for writing. In a **description**, an author tells **details** about one thing after another.

▶ Answer the questions about **Who Put the Cookies in the Cookie Jar?**

🔍 Pages 158–161 What is the author describing? How does the way the author organizes the information help you?

_____

- - - - - - - - - - - - - - - - - - - -

_____

- - - - - - - - - - - - - - - - - - - -

_____

🔍 Pages 166–169 Why did the author write this text? How does the way he organized the information help you?

_____

- - - - - - - - - - - - - - - - - - - -

_____

- - - - - - - - - - - - - - - - - - - -

_____

Name _____

Phonics Review

One **vowel** followed by a **consonant** usually has a short vowel sound. The word **up** has a **short u** sound. The word **on** has a **short o** sound. The word **it** has a **short i** sound.

▶ Write the word that completes each sentence.

1. Jon can sip from a __cup__ .

   (cup)   cap   cut

2. This dog likes to __yip__ .

   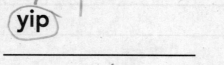

   yum   yes   (yip)

3. Val can run and __win__ .

   wag   (win)   wig

4. Vic got on the __bus__ .

   but   bud   (bus)

5. Jan did a good __job__ .

   (job)   jig   jug

Name _____

Words About Actions and Directions

Action words tell what someone or something is doing. Action words are called **verbs**. **Direction words** tell where a person or thing is moving or going.

▶ Underline the action word in each sentence. Draw a circle around the direction word. Use a dictionary to find the meanings of any words you don't know.

1. Bees buzz around flowers.

2. Mice peek under a door.

3. Rabbits hop up a hill.

4. We turn left to go home.

5. They run over the grass.

6. Frogs jump across a log.

Name _____

Words to Know

Learn these words. You will see them in your reading and use them in your writing.

Word Bank

day	every	fly	have
look	made	they	write

▶ Circle the word that best completes each sentence.

1. Val and Rob like to run (look, (every)) day.

2. They ((have,) write) fun in the sun.

3. The kids ((look,) they) up.

4. They see a bug. It is a (day, (fly)).

5. Rob (have, (made)) a hat for Val.

6. She will (made, (write)) VAL on the hat.

Name _____

Short e

You can spell the **short e** sound with e, as in **hen**.

▶ Write each Basic and Review Spelling Word in the correct column.

Words with short e	Words with short u
wet	nut
hen	tub
yet	mud
leg	bug
web	
pen	

Name _____

Consonants *qu*, *x*, *z*; Short *e*

▶ Name each picture. Write the letter or letters for the beginning sound.

 _____
x

 _____
qu

 _____
z

▶ Now write the letter for the ending sound.

 _____
x

 _____
e

 _____
x

The word **ten** has the **short e** vowel sound. The letter **e** stands for that sound.

▶ If a picture name has the **short e** sound, write **e**. (One word does **not** have **short e**, so leave it blank!)

b _e_ d

m __ t

w _e_ b

Name _____

Short *e*

You can spell the **short e** sound with **e**, as in **web**.

▶ Write the Basic Spelling Word that names each picture.

Spelling Words

Basic

yet

web

pen

wet

leg

hen

Review

nut

tub

mud

bug

1. leg

2.  wet

3. 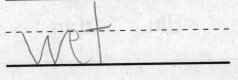 web

4.  pen

5.  hen

▶ Which Basic Spelling Word did you **not** use?
Circle it in the list. Then say a sentence that uses the word.

Name _____

Phonics Review

When a word has only one vowel sound followed by a consonant, the vowel sound is usually short. The words **yet**, **quit**, **fox**, and **mud** all have short vowel sounds.

▶ Write two words to complete each sentence.

1. The ____fox____ is in its ____den____ .

    (fox)   fix   din   (den)

2. Max ____hid____ in a ____box____ .

    lid   (hid)   (box)   pot

3. Meg can ____zip____ the ____top____ .

    zap   (top)   (zip)   tip

4. My ____pup____ got in the ____mud____ .

    (mud)   mad   pep   (pup)

5. A ____yak____ is ____big____ .

    yet   (yak)   (big)   beg

Name _____

Power Words: Match

Word Bank

empty	exclaimed	soon
surprise	twigs	warm

▶ Write the Power Word from **The Nest** that best fits each item.

1. This word means the opposite of **later**.

   soon

2. Which word names something you did not know about?

   surprise

3. Which word means almost the same as **yelled**?

   exclaimed

4. Which word means **small sticks**?

   twigs

5. This word means **not full**.

   empty

6. Which word means **not too hot**?

   warm

Name _____

Words About Time and Position

Time words tell **when** something happens. **Position words** tell **where** something or someone is.

▶ Write a word from the box to finish each sentence. Draw a circle to tell if the word names a **time** or a **position**. Find any words you do not know in a dictionary.

```
┌─────────────────── Word Bank ───────────────────┐
│                                                  │
│  tonight      morning        on        around    │
│                                                  │
└──────────────────────────────────────────────────┘
```

1. I eat toast every __morning__ .

   (time)   position

2. My cap is __on__ my head.

   time   (position)

3. We walked all __around__ the city.

   time   (position)

4. It may rain __tonight__ .

   (time)   position

Name _____

Story Structure

Authors tell the **events** in a story in **sequence.** Describing the important events that happen at the beginning, middle, and end of a story helps readers understand the story better. The words **first, next,** and **last** are used to tell the story events in order.

▶ Answer the questions about **The Nest.**

🔍 Pages 16–19 What happens at the beginning of the story?

_____

- -

_____

- -

_____

🔍 Pages 25 and 30 What happens in the middle and at the end of the story? Which words help tell when the events happen?

_____

- -

_____

- -

_____

Name _____

Synonyms

Synonyms are words that mean the same or almost the same thing.

▶ Read each sentence. Choose the word from the box that means almost the same as the underlined word. Write it on the line.

Word Bank

| loud | happy | wet | small |

1. My hat is <u>damp</u> from the rain.

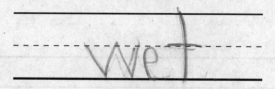
wet

2. The barking dog is so <u>noisy</u>!

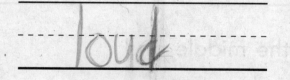
loud

3. My shoes are too <u>tiny</u>.

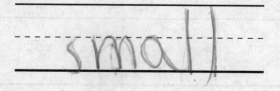
small

4. We were <u>glad</u> to see our friends.

happy

Name _____

Ask and Answer Questions

When you have a discussion, you can **ask and answer questions** to make sure you understand a word, a book, or a topic. You can also ask questions to get help to do something or to get more information.

Remember these important rules:

- Listen with care.
- Stay on topic.
- Give enough information when answering questions.
- Use complete sentences.
- Be respectful.

▶ Follow the rules above as you discuss **Animal Q & A** with a partner. Then mark each rule that you followed.

1. What questions can you ask about the text?

_____

- - - - - - - - - - - - - - - - - - - -

_____

- - - - - - - - - - - - - - - - - - - -

_____

- - - - - - - - - - - - - - - - - - - -

_____

2. What can you do to find answers to your
questions?

_____

- -

_____

- -

_____

- -

_____

3. Which rules did you follow in your discussion?
Put a check in the box next to each rule
you followed.

☐ I listened with care.

☐ I stayed on topic.

☐ I gave enough information when I
answered the questions.

☐ I used complete sentences.

☐ I was respectful.

Name _____

Words to Know

Word Bank

all	down	four	from
her	now	saw	went

▶ Write a word from the box to complete each sentence.

1. Kim _____saw_____ a bug.

2. The bug had _____four_____ dots.

3. Kim got a box from _____her_____ mom.

4. She put the box _____down_____ .

5. The bug _____went_____ in her box.

▶ Think of a sentence about what might happen next. Use at least one word from the Word Bank. Tell your sentence to a partner.

Name _____

Double Final Consonants

Some short vowel words end with two consonants that stand for one sound. For example, the letters **gg** in **egg** stand for one sound, /g/.

▶ Write each Basic Spelling Word in the correct column.

Words with **ll**	Words with **ss**	Other words
will	grass	egg
tell	miss	wet
well		yet
		leg

Basic

will
egg
grass
tell
miss
well

Review

wet
yet
leg
web

Name _____

Double Final Consonants

The word **muff** has the double final consonants **ff**. Double final consonants stand for one sound. If a word has one vowel, and it is followed by double consonants, the vowel sound is usually short. The word **muff** has the **short u** sound.

▶ Name each picture. Write the double consonants that stand for the ending sound.

| **dd** | **ff** | **ll** | **ss** | **zz** |

hi ll

gra ss

a dd

we ll

bu zz

be ll

pu ll

ki ss

cu ff

Name _____

Double Final Consonants

Some short vowel words end with two consonants that stand for one sound. For example, the letters **ss** in **grass** stand for one sound, **/s/**.

▶ Write the Basic Spelling Word that best completes each sentence.

1. Are you sick or ___*well*___ ?

2. The hen sits on her ___*leg*___ .

3. I do not ___*miss*___ when I am at bat.

4. He cut the ___*grass*___ .

5. Can you ___*tell*___ me your name?

6. I ___*will*___ fix up my bed.

Spelling Words

Basic

will

egg

grass

tell

miss

well

Review

wet

yet

leg

web

Vocabulary

Name _____

Power Words: Yes or No?

Word Bank

dull   thank   once

▶ Read each sentence. Circle **YES** if the word makes sense or **NO** if it does not. Rewrite the sentence so it makes sense.

1. I will **thank** Mom for my new hat.

(YES)   NO

_____

_____

2. The yellow bus is a **dull** color.

YES   (NO)

The yellow bus is a bright color

3. I will go to bed **once** I wake up.

YES   (NO)

I will go to bed once i go to sleep.

Point of View

When authors choose a **narrator**, they decide from which **point of view** they will tell the story. If a story is told from the first-person point of view, a character in the story is the narrator. If a story is told from the third-person point of view, the narrator is not a character in the story.

▶ Answer the questions about **Blue Bird and Coyote.**

🔍 Pages 44-45 Is the narrator a character in the story? How do you know?

_____
- -
_____
- -
_____

🔍 Page 48 From which point of view is this story told? How do you know?

_____
- -
_____
- -
_____

Name _____

Phonics Review

Double final consonants stand for one sound as in the word **bill**. The consonants **ck** stand for one sound as in the word **back**. If a word has one vowel, and it is followed by two consonants, the vowel sound is usually short.

▶ Choose and write the word that completes each sentence.

1. A cat will __hiss__ at a dog.

    has   (hiss)   his

2. You can hop __add__ a dock.

    off   odd   (add)

3. Jill can __pack__ her bag.

    peck   pass   (pack)

4. That bug likes to __buzz__.

    bus   (buzz)   back

Name _____

Words About Time and Position

Time words tell **when** something happens. **Position words** tell **where** something or someone is.

▶ Choose the word that best completes each sentence. Write the word on the line. Then circle **when** or **where** to tell if it is a **time word** or a **position word**.

Word Bank			
through	always	tomorrow	above

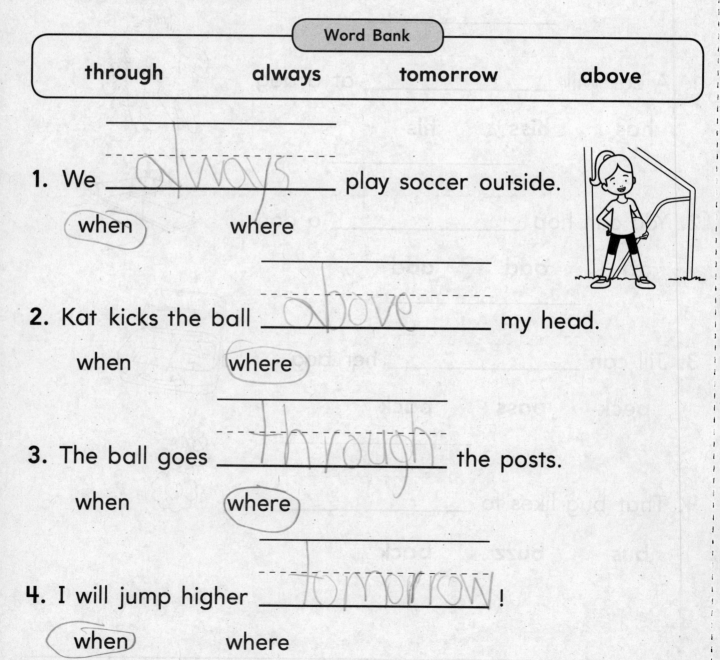

1. We _____*always*_____ play soccer outside.

   (when)   where

2. Kat kicks the ball _____*above*_____ my head.

   when   (where)

3. The ball goes _____*through*_____ the posts.

   when   (where)

4. I will jump higher _____*tomorrow*_____!

   (when)   where

Name _____

Power Words: Draw and Write

Word Bank

shingle   shriek   stroll

▶ Draw a picture or write words that will help you remember each Power Word from **Have You Heard the Nesting Bird?** Try to write more than you draw.

1. shingle

2. shriek

3. stroll

Name _____

Text Organization

Authors choose a **text organization**, or way to arrange information, that fits their reason for writing. In a **description**, an author tells **details** about one thing after another.

▶ Answer the questions about **Have You Heard the Nesting Bird?**

🔍 Pages 62–63 How does the author organize the information? Why do you think she does this?

_____

- -

_____

_____

- -

_____

🔍 Pages 68–69 What does the author want you to learn? How does she organize the information?

_____

- -

_____

_____

- -

_____

Name _____

Words to Know

▶ Write the word from the box that best completes each sentence.

1. Pam and Dan ___know___ how to run.

2. They ___call___ out to Rex.

3. "He ___would___ run with us," Pam says.

4. We can have ___some___ fun.

5. Rex runs ___by___ Pam and Dan.

6. They ___were___ not as quick as Rex.

7. Jill ___would___ like to run, too.

Name _____

Consonant Digraph *sh*

You can spell the /**sh**/ sound with **sh**, as in **ship**.

▶ Write each Basic Spelling Word in the correct column.

<table>
<tr><th>Words beginning
with *sh*</th><th>Words ending
with *sh*</th></tr>
<tr><td>ship</td><td>rush</td></tr>
<tr><td>shop</td><td>fish</td></tr>
<tr><td>dash</td><td>dash</td></tr>
<tr><td>wish</td><td>wish</td></tr>
</table>

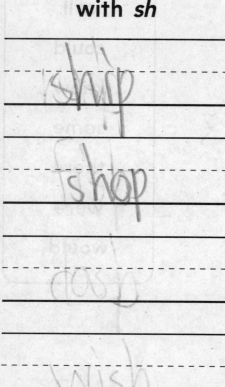
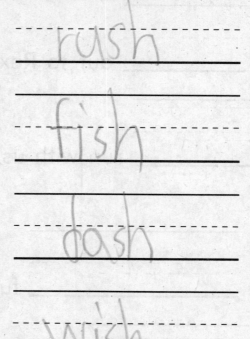

Spelling Words

Basic

ship

shop

wish

rush

fish

dash

Review

grass

miss

will

tell

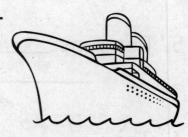

Name _____

Consonant Digraph *sh*

Sometimes, two consonant letters together stand for one sound. The consonant letters **sh** stand for one sound. They stand for the sound at the beginning of **ship**. They also stand for the sound at the end of **wish**.

▶ Name each picture. Choose and write the word that names the picture.

sell   (shell)   *shell*

fish   fizz   *fish*

(ship)   sip   *ship*

cats   (cash)   *cash*

(shop)   hop   *shop*

(dish)   dash   *dish*

Name _____

Consonant Digraph *sh*

You can spell the /sh/ sound with **sh**, as in **fish**.

▶ Read each clue. Unscramble the word. Write the Spelling Word correctly on the line.

Basic

ship

shop

wish

rush

fish

dash

Review

grass

miss

will

tell

1. Run fast   **ahds**   *dash*

2. Look to buy   **ophs**   *shop*

3. Go fast   **hsru**   *rush*

4. Want to have   **siwh**   *wish*

5. Big boat   **ihps**   *ships*

6. A wet pet   **ihsf**   *fish*

Name _____

Power Words: Match

Word Bank

circling   herd   predators   prey   school

▶ Write the Power Word from **Step-by-Step Advice from the Animal Kingdom** that best fits each item.

1. Which word means almost the same as **hunters**?

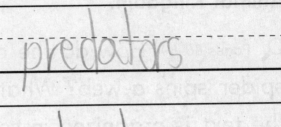
predators

2. Which word names a group of fish?

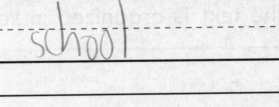
school

3. This word means to move animals in a group.

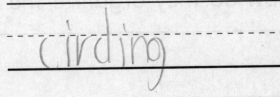
prey

4. This word names animals that get hunted by other animals.

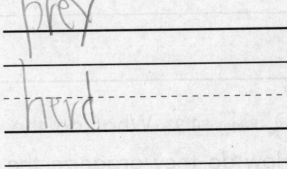
herd

5. Which word means to go around and around?

circling

Name _____

Text Organization

Authors choose a **text organization**, or structure, that fits the topic and their reason for writing. **Chronological order** tells about events in sequence. **Graphic features**, like numbers, can help readers know how a text is organized.

▶ Answer the questions about **Step-by-Step Advice from the Animal Kingdom**.

🔍 Pages 86–89 How do the authors explain how a spider spins a web? What clues help you know that the text is organized in sequence?

_____

- - - - - - - - - - - - - - - - - - - -

_____

- - - - - - - - - - - - - - - - - - - -

_____

🔍 Pages 90–92 What do the authors want you to learn? How do they organize the information?

_____

- - - - - - - - - - - - - - - - - - - -

_____

- - - - - - - - - - - - - - - - - - - -

_____

Name _____

Phonics Review

The consonant letter **s** stands for the sound at the beginning of **sip**. The consonant letters **sh** together stand for the sound at the beginning of **ship**.

▶ Choose and write the word that completes each sentence.

1. We can buy jam at this __shop__ .

   shot　　**shut**　　**shop**

2. The van ran out of __gas__ .

   gas　　**gash**　　**gush**

3. The cat can __sip__ from the dish.

   ship　　**sip**　　**sis**

4. Sal has on her red __socks__ .

   socks　　**shock**　　**sick**

5. Jess has six pet __fish__ .

   fizz　　**fits**　　**fish**

Name _____

Inflection *–ing*

A **verb** is an action word. The **ending –ing** can be added to a verb to tell when something is happening.

▶ Choose the word that best completes each sentence. Write the word on the line.

1. We are ___*planting*___ a seed.

   plant   (planting)

2. Lee is ___*watering*___ it now.

   watering   water

3. I can ___*help*___ too!

   (help)   helping

4. It will start ___*growing*___ soon!

   grow   (growing)

▶ Take turns with a partner. Tell the meaning of the word you picked. Tell why it fits the sentence.

Name _____

Words to Know

Knowing how to read and write these words can make you a better reader and writer.

Word Bank

be	here	me	play
started	today	use	very

▶ Write a word from the box to complete each sentence.

1. My pal Nick is __here__ today.

2. I like to __play__ with Nick.

3. He is __very__ fun.

4. Nick will __be__ first.

5. He will kick the ball to __me__ .

6. I __started__ my legs to run.

91

Name _____

Consonant Digraph *ch*

You can spell the /ch/ sound with **ch** at the beginning of a word, as in **chick**, or at the end of a word, as in **rich**.

▶ Write each Spelling Word in the correct column.

<table>
<tr><th>Words that
begin with *ch*</th><th>Words that
end with *ch*</th></tr>
<tr><td>chin</td><td>much</td></tr>
<tr><td>chop</td><td>rich</td></tr>
<tr><td>chip</td><td></td></tr>
<tr><td>chick</td><td></td></tr>
</table>

Spelling Words

Basic

chin
chop
much
chip
rich
chick

Review

shop
wish
rush
ship

Name _____

Consonant Digraph *ch*

The consonants **ch** together stand for the sound at the beginning of **chip**.

When a word has one **vowel** that is followed by one or two **consonants**, the vowel usually has a short sound.

▶ Write the word that names the picture. Use **chick, check**.

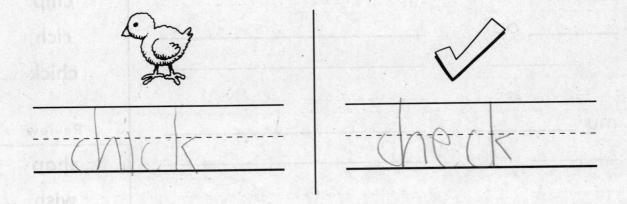

chick   check

The words **much**, **rich**, and **such** end with the sound for **ch**. When a word has one **vowel** that is followed by one or two **consonants**, the vowel usually has a short sound.

▶ Write a sentence. Use **much, rich, such**.

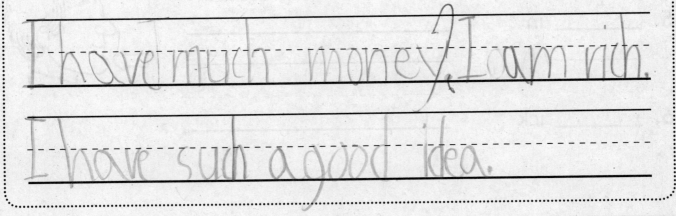

I have much money. I am rich.

I have such a good idea.

Name _____

Consonant Digraph *ch*

You can spell the /**ch**/ sound with **ch** at the beginning of a word, as in **chin**, or at the end of a word, as in **much**.

▶ Write the missing letters. Then write the Spelling Word on the line.

Spelling Words

Basic

chin

chop

much

chip

rich

chick

Review

shop

wish

rush

ship

1. 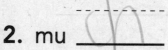 op    *chop*

2. mu 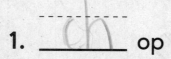   *much*

3. 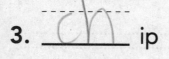 ip   *chip*

4. ri 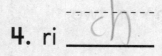   *rich*

5. 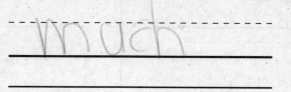 in   *chin*

6.  ick   *chick*

Name _____

Phonics Review

Digraphs: The consonants **ch** stand for the sound in **chip** and **much**. The consonants **sh** stand for the sound in **shop** and **dash**.
Trigraph: The consonants **shr** stand for the first sounds in **shred**.

▶ Write words with **ch, sh,** and **shr** to make rhymes. Use the words in the box.

chill	cash	such	mush
chat	shack	shrub	dish

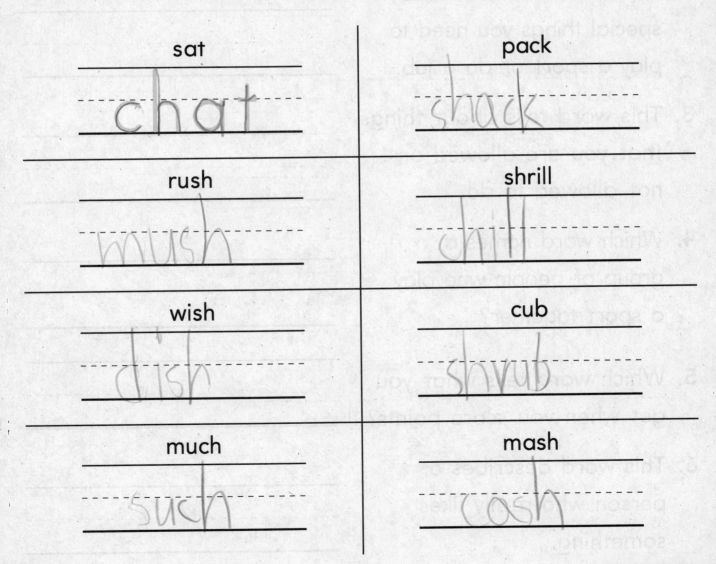

sat

chat

pack

shack

rush

mush

shrill

chill

wish

dish

cub

shrub

much

such

mash

cash

Name _____

Power Words: Match

Word Bank

| coach | equipment | fan | goal | rules | team |

▶ Write the Power Word from **Goal!** that best fits each item.

1. This word means to teach a game or sport.

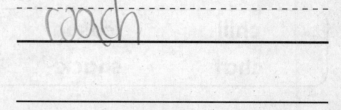

2. This word tells about the special things you need to play a sport or do a job.

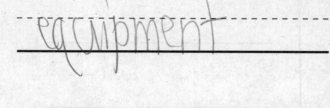

3. This word tells about things that you are allowed or not allowed to do.

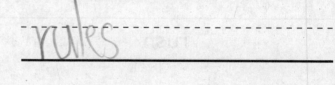

4. Which word names a group of people who play a sport together?

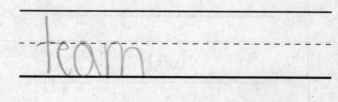

5. Which word tells what you get when you score points?

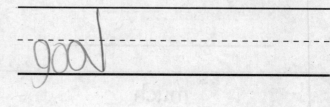

6. This word describes a person who really likes something.

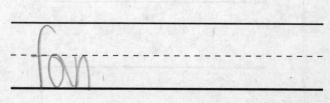

Name _____

Compound Words

Compound words are words made up of two smaller words. Use the meaning of the smaller words to figure out the meaning of the compound word.

▶ Circle the compound word in each sentence. Then write the two smaller words that make up each compound word.

1. Max likes his doghouse.

_____dog_____   _____house_____

2. I have a new lunchbox.

_____lunch_____   _____box_____

3. We found a starfish in the sea.

_____star_____   _____fish_____

4. Did you ring the doorbell?

_____door_____   _____bell_____

Name _____

Point of View

When authors choose a **narrator** for a text, they decide from whose **point of view** they will tell it. If the author tells a text from a first-person point of view, the narrator is a person in the text and uses words like **I**, **my**, and **me**. If the author tells a text from a third-person point of view, the narrator is not a person in the text. An outside narrator can tell about all the people in the text and uses words like **he**, **she**, and **they**.

▶ Answer the questions about **Goal!**

🔍 Pages 114–115 Who is the narrator? How do you know?

_____

- -

_____

_____

- -

_____

🔍 Pages 124–125 From which point of view is this text told? Which words help you understand this?

_____

- -

_____

_____

- -

_____

Name _____

Context Clues

When you come to a word you do not know, you can use **context clues** to figure out what it means. Look around the word you do not know for hints about what it means.

▶ Read each sentence below. Circle the clues that help you know the meaning of the underlined word. Then circle the meaning.

1. The glow of the bright moon helps people see at night.

   (light)   dark

2. You can make food on a hot blaze for dinner.

   (fire)   pan

3. Plants need sun to grow and stay alive.

   (living)   yellow

4. The sun comes out at dawn every morning.

   (beginning of day)   end of day

Give and Follow Instructions

Instructions are directions that tell how to make or do something. **Sequence words**, such as **first**, **next**, and **last**, help explain the order of the steps when giving instructions and understand the steps when following instructions.

► Write instructions below for how to make or do something. Use sequence words.

_____

- -

_____

- -

_____

- -

_____

► Read the instructions you wrote to a partner. Then answer the questions.

Did you speak clearly?	YES	NO
Did you tell the steps in order?	YES	NO
Did you use sequence words?	YES	NO
Did you repeat the instructions?	YES	NO

Name _____

What else did you do? _____

_____

_____

_____

▶ Listen to your partner's instructions. Then answer
the questions.

Did you listen carefully?	YES	NO
Did you hear any sequence words?	YES	NO
Did you ask questions about the steps?	YES	NO
Did you repeat the instructions?	YES	NO

What else did you do? _____

_____

_____

_____

Name _____

Words to Know

▶ Write the word that best completes each sentence.

1. Meg and Nan ___say___ ,
   "We want to play!"

2. ___Where___ can they go?

3. They can ___walk___ to the hill.

4. Do they know the ___way___
   to the hill?

5. Yes! They go the ___right___ way.

6. Meg and Nan ___jump___ and run.

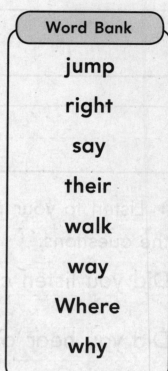

Word Bank

jump

right

say

their

walk

way

Where

why

Name _____

Consonant Digraphs *th*, *wh*

You can spell the /th/ sound with **th**, as in **that**.
You can spell the /hw/ sound with **wh**, as in **whip**.

▶ Write each Basic Spelling Word in the correct column.

Words with *th*	Words with *wh*
that	which
this	whip
then	

Name _____

Consonant Digraphs *th*, *wh*; Trigraph *–tch*

The letters **th** can stand for the first sound in **this** or **thin**. The letters **wh** stand for the first sound in **when**. The letters **thr** (a trigraph) stand for the first two sounds in **thrill**.

▶ Name each picture. Write the letters that stand for what you hear at the beginning. Use **th**, **wh**, or **thr**.

Throne | Thumb | whale

The consonants **th** can stand for the sound at the end of **bath**. The consonants **tch** stand for the sound at the end of **catch**.

▶ Write **bath** or **catch** to complete each sentence.

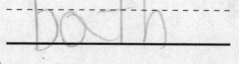

1. The dog needs a _____bath_____ .

2. First, we have to _____catch_____ him.

Name _____

Consonant Digraphs *th*, *wh*

You can spell the /th/ sound with **th**, as in **then**.
You can spell the /hw/ sound with **wh**, as in **which**.

▶ Read each word. Write the Basic Spelling Words that rhyme with it.

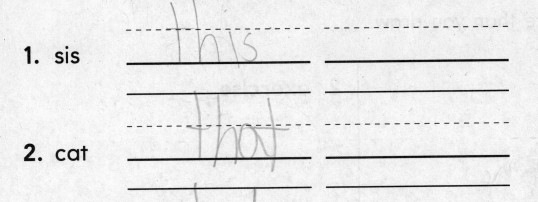

1. sis   *this*   _____

2. cat   *that*   _____

3. rich   *which*   _____

4. hen   *then*   _____

Spelling Words
Basic
that
with
this
then
whip
which
Review
much
chick
rich
chin

▶ Which Basic Spelling Words did you **not** use?
Circle them in the list. Then say a sentence that
uses each word.

Name _____

Power Words: Draw and Write

Word Bank

| body | exercise | well |

▶ Draw a picture or write words that will help you remember each Power Word from **Get Up and Go!** Try to write more than you draw.

1. body

2. exercise

3. well

Name _____

Text Features

Text features help authors explain ideas and readers locate information. **Charts** let readers see and understand information. **Headings** structure the text into different parts. **Special text** in different colors and sizes calls attention to that text.

▶ Answer the questions about **Get Up and Go!**

🔍 Page 138 What information does the heading give? Why does the author use different colors and sizes of text?

_____

- -

_____

- -

_____

- -

🔍 Page 144 What does this chart tell you? What do you learn from this chart?

_____

- -

_____

- -

Name _____

Phonics Review

The consonants **th** stand for the first sound in **this** and the last sound in **path**. The consonants **wh** stand for the first sound in **when**. The consonants **tch** stand for the last sound in **pitch**.

You can add **–s** or **–es** to a word to name more than one.

▶ Write the words to complete the sentences.

patch   **patches**

One cat has a ___patch___ on its back.

One cat has six ___patches___ .

path   **paths**

I see two ___paths___ .

Which ___path___ do we take?

Name _____

Compound Words

Compound words are words made up of two smaller words. Use the meaning of the smaller words to figure out the meaning of the compound word.

▶ Choose two words from the box to make a compound word that completes each sentence. Write the compound word on the line. Use a dictionary to find the meanings of any words you don't know.

> **Word Bank**
>
> flowers   bug   yard   back
>
> sun   butter   lady   fly

1. We plant a garden in our ___back yard___ .

2. We saw a beautiful ___butterfly___ .

3. The ___sunflowers___ grow tall.

4. A ___lady bug___ rests on a leaf.

Power Words: Yes or No?

Word Bank

hero   excuse   guy

▶ Read each sentence. Circle **YES** if the word or
words in bold make sense or **NO** if they do not.
Rewrite the sentence so it makes sense.

1. A **hero** can be a **guy** or a girl.

(YES)   NO

_____

- - - - - - - - - - - - - - - - - - -

_____

- - - - - - - - - - - - - - - - - - -

_____

2. It is bad manners to say **excuse** me.

YES   (NO)

It is good manners to
say excuse me.

Name _____

Characters

A **character** is the person, animal, or thing a story is about. Readers get to know the characters by looking for clues in the words and pictures. Understanding characters helps readers describe them and the **reasons** for their **actions**.

▶ Answer the questions about **A Big Guy Took My Ball!**

🔍 Pages 158–163 What do you know about the characters? Why does Gerald go get Piggie's ball?

_____

- -

_____

- -

_____

- -

_____

🔍 Pages 176–180 Why do Gerald and Piggie ask the big guy to play? How do you know?

_____

- -

_____

- -

_____

Name _____

Words to Know

Word Bank

after	before	does	don't
grow	into	no	wash

▶ Circle the word that best completes each sentence.

1. My dog (does, into) not want a bath.

2. I will (grow, wash) her.

3. I will do it (after, don't) I eat.

4. She runs, but I tell her (no, does).

5. I put her (before, into) the tub.

6. One day she will (grow, don't) too big for it.

7. My dog was a mess (before, after) her bath.

8. I (don't, wash) know how she does it!

Name _____

Initial Blends with *s*

You can spell the **/st/** sound with **st**, as in **stop**.
You can spell the **/sp/** sound with **sp**, as in **spit**.
You can spell the **/sl/** sound with **sl**, as in **slid**.

Some blends are spelled with three letters (trigraphs). You can spell the **/str/** sound with **str**, as in **strap**. You can spell the **/spl/** sound with **spl**, as in **split**.

▶ Write each Basic Spelling Word in the correct column.

Words with *st* or *str*	Words with *sp* or *spl*	Words with *sl*
stop	spit	slid
step	split	
strap	spit	

Spelling Words
Basic
stop
step
strap
spit
split
slid
Review
this
whip
which
that

Name _____

Initial Blends with *s*

Two or three letters together can form a **consonant blend**.
Each letter keeps its own sound. The sounds are close together.
The words **stop**, **slip**, **smash**, **snack**, **skip**, and **spell** begin
with **s** blends. **Splat** and **strum** have 3-letter blends (trigraphs).

▶ Name each picture. Write the blend that begins each
picture name. Use these blends: **sk, sl, sm, sn, sp, str.**

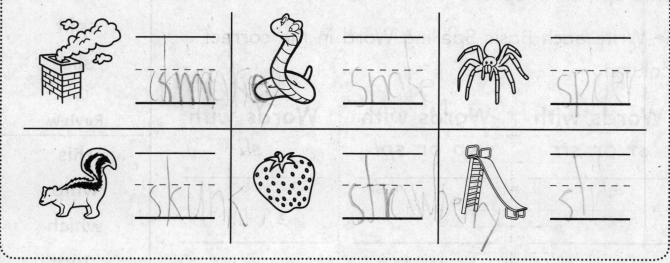

▶ Choose and write the word that names each picture.

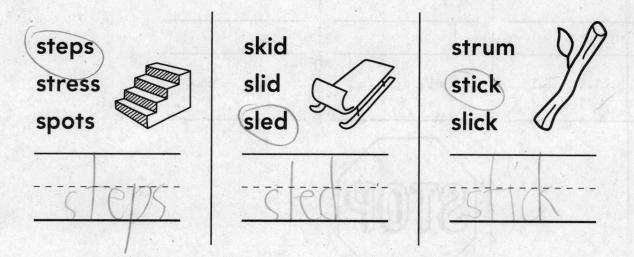

steps
stress
spots

skid
slid
sled

strum
stick
slick

Initial Blends with *s*

You can spell the /st/ sound with **st**, as in **step**.
You can spell the /sp/ sound with **sp**, as in **spit**.
You can spell the /sl/ sound with **sl**, as in **slid**.

Some blends are spelled with three letters (trigraphs). You can spell the /str/ sound with **str** and the /spl/ sound with **spl**.

▶ Write the Spelling Word that best completes each sentence.

Spelling Words
Basic
stop
step
strap
spit
split
slid
Review
this
whip
which
that

1. You can ___split___ the chips.

2. They ___slid___ down the hill.

3. I will ___step___ out the pit.

4. The house has one ___step___ up.

5. The van will ___stop___ and not go.

6. The ___strap___ on the bag is red.

Name _____

Power Words: Match

```
                    Word Bank
   trouble    seed      fruits     heap      short
```

▶ Write the Power Word from **If You Plant a Seed** that best fits each item.

1. This word names part of a plant that grows into a new plant.

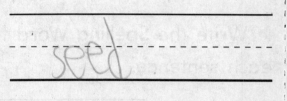

2. Which word means almost the same as **pile**?

3. Which word describes something you get from hard work?

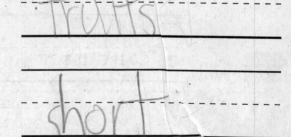

4. This word means **not lasting very long**.

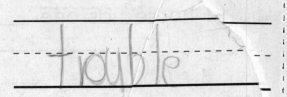

5. Which word means almost the same as **a problem**?

116

Name _____

Theme

The **topic** is what a story is mostly about. The **theme** is the big idea about the topic. The lesson, or **moral**, is what the author wants readers to take away from the story. Look for the lesson to help you figure out a story's theme.

▶ Answer the questions about **If You Plant a Seed**.

🔍 Pages 198–201 Why are the animals fighting? What is this part of the story mostly about?

_____

- -

_____

- -

_____

🔍 Pages 203–208 What is this story mostly about? What does the author want you to learn?

_____

- -

_____

- -

_____

- -

_____

Name _____

Phonics Review

The consonants **th** stand for the first sound in **thick** and the last sound in **path**. The consonants **sh** stand for the first sound in **shed** and the last sound in **mash**.

In a consonant blend, 2 or 3 (trigraph) consonants keep their own sounds, but you say them closely together. The words **stop**, **slip**, **smash**, **snack**, **skip**, **spell**, **just**, **splash**, and **strap** have **s** blends.

▶ Write words that rhyme. Use the words in the box.

Word Bank
stop   splash   strum   thick   last   skip

mop	slick
stop	thick
ship	fast
skip	last
hum	cash
strum	splash

Name _____

Suffixes *–er*, *–est*

A **suffix** is a word part that comes at the end of a base word. The **suffixes –er** and **–est** are added to adjectives to make words that are used to compare.

▶ Read each sentence. Circle the word that completes the sentence and write it on the line. Look up any base words you do not know in the dictionary.

1. A snail is _____slower_____ than a turtle.

   slowest   (**slower**)

2. January was the _____coldest_____ month last year.

   cold   (**coldest**)

3. An apple is _____sweeter_____ than a lemon.

   sweet   (**sweeter**)

Name _____

Words to Know

Learn these words. You will see them in your reading and use them in your writing.

(**Word Bank**)

around	came	come	found
other	people	two	worked

▶ Write a word from the box to complete each sentence.

1. My ____two____ pals are Jack and Jan.

2. We ____came____ here to play.

3. Will you ____come____ and play with us?

4. There are many other ____people____ here.

▶ Write a sentence that uses one new word from the box.

_____

_____

_____

Grade 1

120

Module 5 • Week 1

Name _____

Initial Blends with /

You can spell the **/fl/** sound with **fl**, as in **flag**.
You can spell the **/cl/** sound with **cl**, as in **club**.
You can spell the **/sl/** sound with **sl**, as in **slam**.

▶ Write each Spelling Word in the correct column.

Words with fl	Words with cl	Words with sl
flap	club	sled
flag	clap	slid
		slam

Name _____

Initial Blends with *l*

Two or three consonants together can form a **consonant blend**. Each consonant keeps its own sound. The sounds are close together. The words **black**, **clap**, **flap**, **glad**, **plan**, **slip**, and **split** all begin with *l* blends.

▶ Name each picture. Write the blend that begins each picture name. Use these blends: **bl**, **cl**, **fl**, **gl**, **pl**, or **spl**.

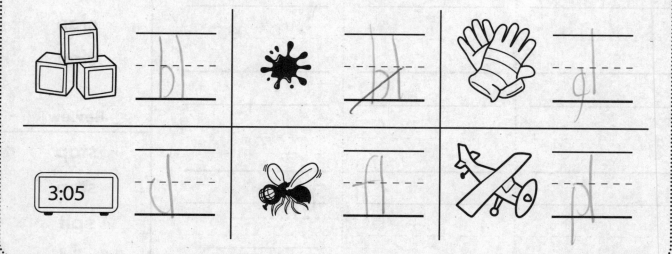

bl   bl   gl

cl   fl   pl

▶ Choose and write the word that names each picture.

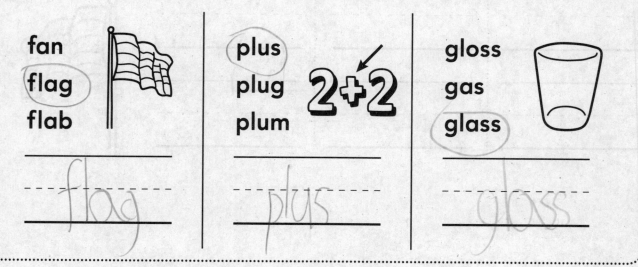

fan
(flag)
flab

_____
flag

plus
plug
plum

_____
plus

gloss
gas
(glass)

_____
glass

Name _____

Initial Blends with l

You can spell the /fl/ sound with **fl**, as in **flap**.
You can spell the /cl/ sound with **cl**, as in **clap**.
You can spell the /sl/ sound with **sl**, as in **slam**.

▶ Read each clue. Unscramble the word.
Write the Spelling Word correctly on the line.

1. You can join this. **cbul** _club_

2. Shut fast. **amls** _slam_

3. Your hands can
   do this. **palc** _clap_

4. Wings do this. **alfp** _flap_

5. Use this on hills. **edls** _sled_

6. Our country has
   one. **lfga** _flag_

Spelling Words
Basic
flap
club
flag
slam
clap
sled
Review
stop
step
spit
slid

Name _____

Phonics Review

Two or three (trigraph) consonants together can form a **consonant blend**. Each consonant keeps its own sound. The sounds are close together. Many consonants can form blends with **s** or **l**. The words **stop** and **strap** have **s** blends. The word **flap** has an **l** blend.

▶ Write the name for each picture. Use the words in the box.

```
┌──────────────────────────────────────────────┐
│                 Word Bank                      │
│   clip     splat     plug     glass    flag   │
│      stem      sled      clock      glad      │
└──────────────────────────────────────────────┘
```

clip	glad	flag
stem	splat	sled
plug	clock	glass

Power Words: Match

$$\boxed{\text{Word Bank}}$$

blackout   busy   huddled   idea   normal   still

▶ Write the Power Word from **Blackout** that best fits each item.

1. Which word means the
   opposite of **stood far apart**?   _huddled_

2. Which word describes how
   you would feel if you had to
   go to school, go to soccer,
   and then go to a party?   _busy_

3. Which word is made up of
   two smaller words?   _blackout_

4. This word means almost the
   same as **calm** and **quiet**.   _still_

5. Which word means the same
   as **thought**?   _idea_

6. This word tells about a
   school day that is the same
   as all the other school days.   _normal_

Name _____

Suffixes –er and –est

A **suffix** is a word part that comes at the end of a base word. The **suffixes –er** and **–est** are added to adjectives to make words that are used to compare.

▶ Choose a word to complete each sentence. Use a dictionary to find the meanings of any words you don't know.

1. Dad is ____stronger____ than Alex.

(**stronger**)   **strongest**

2. Jing is the ____fastest____ on the team.

faster   (fastest)

3. The rock is ____heavier____ than the box.

(**heavier**)   **heaviest**

4. That clown is the ____funniest____ of all.

funnier   (funniest)

Name _____

Story Structure

Authors use **story structure** to organize their stories. The beginning of the story usually explains the **problem**. The **events** in the middle tell how the characters try to solve the problem. The end explains the **resolution**, or how the problem is solved. These events make up the story's **plot**.

▶ Answer the questions about **Blackout**.

🔍 Pages 20–25 What is the main problem? How do the characters react to the problem?

_____

- -

_____

🔍 Pages 27–36 Can you use **first** to state the problem? Use **next** and **last** to discuss how the characters resolved the problem.

_____

- -

_____

_____

- -

_____

Name _____

Reference Sources

You can find the meaning of a word you don't know in a **dictionary** or **glossary**. The words are in **alphabetical order**. This order is the same as the letters in the alphabet.

▶ Write the words in alphabetical order. Then circle one word in each group. Look up the word in a dictionary and write its meaning.

1. mess, dab, hem

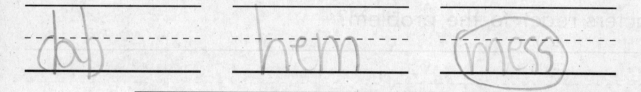

Meaning: _____

_____

2. puff, poke, pal

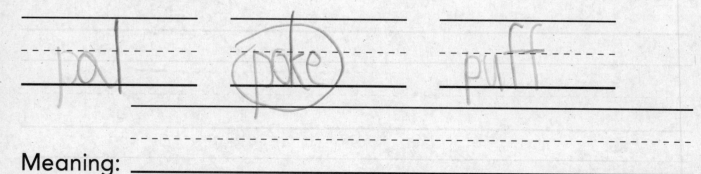

Meaning: _____

_____

Name _____

Digital Tools

Digital tools are types of **technology** that are used for research, like computers, tablets, and smartphones. We use these tools to help us find information. Other tools help us create and display **presentations** in which we can share information with others.

▶ Look at the website below. Then answer the questions.

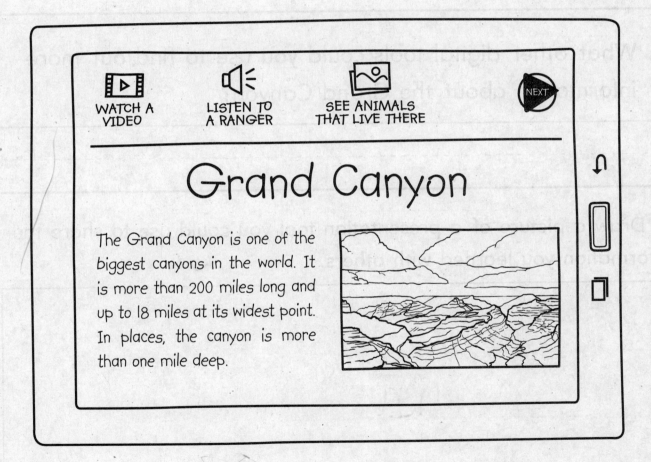

Grade 1

Name _____

1. What does this website tell about?

_____

- -

_____

2. What would you tap on if you wanted to listen to a ranger talking about the Grand Canyon?

_____

- -

_____

3. What other digital tools could you use to find out more information about the Grand Canyon?

_____

- -

_____

▶ Draw a picture of a presentation tool you could use to share the information you learned with others.

Name _____

Words to Know

▶ Write the word that best completes each sentence.

1. It is _____cold_____ and wet today.

2. I put on my hat _____because_____ it is cold.

3. It is a _____pretty_____ hat!

4. Will I go out _____or_____ play here?

5. I do not want to _____cold_____ and get wet.

6. I want the sun to come out _____again_____ !

Initial Blends with *r*

You can spell the **/dr/** sound with **dr**, as in **drum**.
You can spell the **/tr/** sound with **tr**, as in **trap**.
You can spell the **/gr/** sound with **gr**, as in **grin**.
You can spell the **/scr/** sound with three letters
(a trigraph), **scr**, as in **scrub**.

▶ Write each Basic Spelling Word in the correct
column.

Words with **dr**	Words with **tr**	Words with **gr**
drip	trap	grin
drum	trip	

▶ Write the word that starts with **scr** and rhymes

with **tub**. ~~dub~~ drum

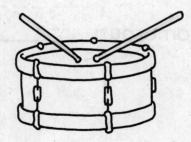

Spelling Words
Basic
drip
trap
drum
trip
grin
scrub
Review
flap
clap
sled
club

Name _____

Initial Blends with *r*

Two or three (trigraph) consonants together can form a **consonant blend**. Each letter keeps its own sound. The sounds are close together. **Brush, crush, sprig, strip,** and **strap** begin with **r** blends.

▶ Name each picture. Write the blend that begins each picture name. Use these blends: **br, fr, gr, scr,** or **str.**

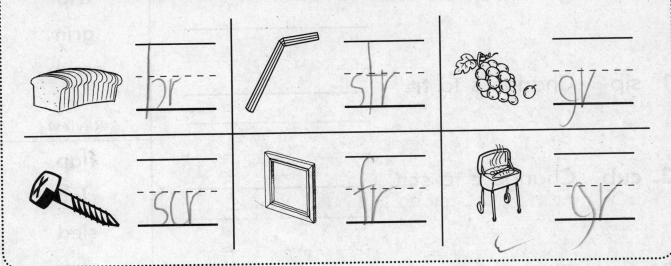

br	str	gr
scr	fr	gr

▶ Write the word that names each picture.

sack
stack
strap

strap

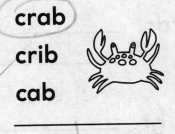

crab
crib
cab

crab

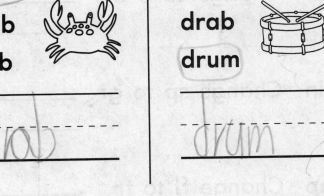

dim
drab
drum

drum

Name _____

Initial Blends with *r*

You can spell the /dr/ sound with **dr**, as in **drum**.
You can spell the /tr/ sound with **tr**, as in **trip**.
You can spell the /gr/ sound with **gr**, as in **grin**.
You can spell the /scr/ sound with three letters
(a trigraph), **scr**, as in **scrub**.

▶ Read each word. Follow the directions. Write
the Spelling Word on the line.

Spelling Words
Basic
drip
trap
drum
trip
grin
scrub
Review
flap
clap
sled
club

1. **sip**   Change **s** to **tr**.   _trip_

2. **cub**   Change **c** to **scr**.   _scrub_

3. **gum**   Change **g** to **dr**.   _drum_

4. **clip**   Change **cl** to **dr**.   _drip_

5. **spin**   Change **sp** to **gr**.   _grin_

6. **flap**   Change **fl** to **tr**.   _trap_

Name _____

Power Words: Draw and Write

Word Bank

| faces | shines | pattern | fades |

▶ Draw a picture or write words that will help you remember each Power Word from **Day and Night**. Try to write more than you draw.

1. faces

2. shines

3. pattern

4. fades

Name _____

Text Features

Authors use text features to help readers locate and understand information. **Diagrams** are pictures that give information. **Labels** on a diagram name its parts. **Headings** tell that a text is structured into different parts and what each part is about. **Photos** are pictures taken with a camera.

▶ Answer the questions about **Day and Night**.

🔍 Page 48 What do the diagram and labels show?

_____

- - - - - - - - - - - - - - - - - - - -

_____

_____

- - - - - - - - - - - - - - - - - - - -

_____

🔍 Page 51 What information does the heading give you? Why do you think the author included photos?

_____

- - - - - - - - - - - - - - - - - - - -

_____

_____

- - - - - - - - - - - - - - - - - - - -

_____

_____

- - - - - - - - - - - - - - - - - - - -

_____

Name _____

Phonics Review

- The words **brush** and **crush** begin with **r** blends. Each consonant keeps its own sound, but you say the sounds closely together.

- A **compound word** is made up of two smaller words. Some compound words have a blend: **dr**um + roll = **dr**umroll.

▶ Name each picture. Circle two words to make a compound word that names the picture. Write the compound word.

	trip trash cram can	trashcan
	back track crack pack	backpack
	drum drip stacks sticks	drumsticks
	glum gum drip drop	gumdrop
	sun drill snip dress	sundress

Name _____

Inflection –s

Sentences have a naming part and an action part. **Verbs** are used in the action part to tell what the person, place, or thing is doing. A verb with the **ending –s** tells about something that is happening to **one** person, place, or thing.

▶ Circle the word that completes the sentence. Tell what it means. Then write the word on the line.

1. Bella ____walks____ to school.

   walk   (walks)

2. The cats ____run____ to the barn.

   (run)   runs

3. Mom ____packs____ a lunch for me.

   pack   (packs)

4. Jess and Anne ____play____ at the park.

   (play)   plays

Name _____

Power Words: Yes or No?

▶ Read each sentence. Circle **YES** if the word makes sense or **NO** if it does not. Rewrite the sentence so it makes sense.

Word Bank

seasons

weather

1. Winter and fall are the hottest **seasons** of the year.

YES   ~~NO~~

Winter and fall are the coldest
seasons of the year

2. We play outside when the **weather** is good.

~~YES~~   NO

Name _____

Ideas and Support

Sometimes authors try to **persuade** readers to do or believe something. They give their **opinion**, or why they believe something. They also give **reasons** to support the opinion. Those reasons are usually facts, or things that can be proved.

▶ Answer the questions about **The Best Season**.

🔍 Pages 66–67 What does the girl want you to think about winter? What reasons does she give to support her opinion?

_____

- -

_____

- -

_____

🔍 Pages 70–71 What does this girl want to persuade you about? What reasons does she give to support her opinion?

_____

- -

_____

- -

_____

Name _____

Words to Know

┌─────────────── Word Bank ───────────────┐

any   done   laugh   long

more   pull   teacher   think

└──┘

▶ Circle the word that best completes each sentence.

1. Ann has a (long, pull), black bug.

2. The kids see it and (laugh, done).

3. Our (teacher, more) does not like bugs.

4. He does not (think, done) bugs are fun.

5. Does Ann have (pull, more) bugs?

6. No, she does not have (long, any) more bugs.

7. We (laugh, pull) out our backpacks.

8. We are (done, any) with class.

Name _____

Final Blends

You can spell the /mp/ sound with **mp**, as in **lamp**.

You can spell the /nt/ sound with **nt**, as in **went**.

You can spell the /st/ sound with **st**, as in **fast**.

▶ Write each Basic Spelling Word in the correct column.

Words with *mp*	Words with *nt*	Words with *st*
jump	went	fast
lamp	ant	must

Spelling Words

Basic

jump

lamp

went

fast

must

ant

Review

trap

drum

trip

grin

Name _____

Final Blends

Two consonants together can form a **consonant blend**.
Each consonant keeps its own sound, but you say the
sounds closely together. The words **help** and **fast** end with
consonant blends. Many different consonants can form blends
at the end of words.

▶ Choose and write the word that names each picture.

gash (gift) gust   limp   laps   (lamp)

gift   _lamp_

(vest) vets   vent   tend   (tent)   test

vest   _tent_

rant   rift (raft)   (plant) plot   plan

raft   _plant_

Name _____

Final Blends

You can spell the **/mp/** sound with **mp**, as in **jump**.
You can spell the **/nt/** sound with **nt**, as in **ant**.
You can spell the **/st/** sound with **st**, as in **must**.

▶ Read each sentence. Cross out the Basic
Spelling Word that is spelled incorrectly. Write it
correctly on the line.

Spelling Words

Basic

jump

lamp

went

fast

must

ant

Review

trap

drum

trip

grin

1. The dog ran fist. _fast_

2. An ent was in the sand. _ant_

3. The cat can junp up. _jump_

4. We mast stop here. _must_

5. I wint to class today. _went_

6. The lemp is on. _lamp_

Power Words: Match

Word Bank

wait   groan   worth   able   wasted

▶ Write the Power Word from **Waiting Is Not Easy!** that best fits each item.

1. Which word would you use to tell about food that was not eaten?

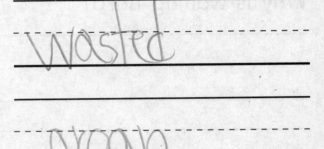

2. Which word tells about a sad sound?

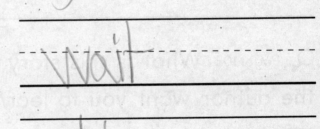

3. Which word tells what you do when you stand in line?

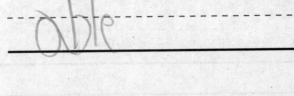

4. This word means you can do something.

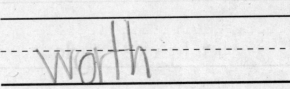

5. Which word means that something is just as good as another thing?

worth

Name _____

Theme

The **topic** of a story is what it is mostly about. The **theme** is the lesson, or **moral**, that the author wants the reader to understand and remember.

▶ Answer the questions about **Waiting Is Not Easy!**

🔍 Pages 94–97 What is Gerald having a hard time doing? Why is waiting hard?

_____
- -
_____
- -
_____

🔍 Page 108 What is this story mostly about? What does the author want you to learn?

_____
- -
_____
- -
_____
- -
_____

Name _____

Phonics Review

The words **help** and **land** end with consonant blends. Each consonant keeps its sound, but you say the consonants closely together.

The **–ed** ending tells that an action happened in the past: I **help** my mom. I **helped** her last week, too.

▶ Write the word that completes each sentence.

1. The cat ___rested___ on the mat.

    (rested)   rented   rusted

2. Mom ___helped___ me make the bed.

    hinted   helped   hunted

3. The frog ___jumped___ in the pond.

    (jumped)   grumped   just

4. My dog ___fetched___ the stick.

    filled   fisted   (fetched)

Name _____

Suffixes –y, –ful

A **suffix** is a word part that comes at the end of a base word. The **suffix –y** means "having or being like something." The **suffix –ful** means "full of."

▶ Circle the words in the box that end with the **suffix –y** or the **suffix –ful**. Then use these words to complete each sentence.

Word Bank

curl	curly	color	colorful
hill	hilly	thank	thankful

1. My dog has very _____ curly _____ hair.

2. She is _____ thankful _____ for the gift.

3. The road was very _____ hilly _____ .

4. My shirt is very _____ colorful _____ .

Name _____

Words to Know

Learn these words. You will see them in your reading and use them in your writing.

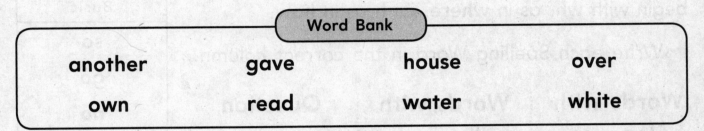

Word Bank

another	gave	house	over
own	read	water	white

▶ Write a word from the box to complete each sentence.

1. This is my _____ .

2. It is a _____ house.

3. I _____ a little dog.

4. My little dog can jump _____ big rocks.

5. I _____ my dog some water.

6. The _____ is very cold.

Name _____

CV Pattern; Question Words

You can spell long vowel sounds with the **consonant-vowel** (CV) pattern, as in **so**. Some question words begin with **wh**, as in **where**, or **h** as in **how**.

▶ Write each Spelling Word in the correct column.

Words with long *o*	Words with long *e*	Question words
So	me	where
go		what
no		what
		when
		why
		how

Spelling Words

Basic

so

go

no

me

where

who

what

when

why

how

Review

fast

lamp

jump

went

Name _____

Long e, i, o (CV)

When there is only one vowel in a word and it is at the end, it usually stands for the long vowel sound. The word **me** has the **long e** vowel sound. The word **so** has the **long o** vowel sound. The word **hi** has the **long i** vowel sound.

▶ Choose and write a word to complete each sentence.

1. My pig used to __be__ big and fat.

   buy   (be)   bet

2. But it has __no__ fluff left in it.

   (no)   so   me

3. I asked Dad if __he__ could add fluff to my pig.

   hi   (he)   hem

4. We did it! Say __hi__ to my old fat pig!

   (hi)   be   hit

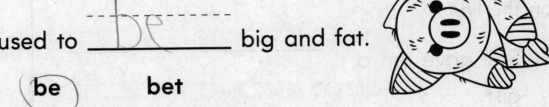

Name _____

CV Pattern; Question Words

You can spell long vowel sounds with the **consonant-vowel** (CV) pattern, as in **go**. Some question words begin with **wh**, as in **what**, or **h**, as in **how**.

▶ Read each sentence. Cross out the Spelling Word that is spelled incorrectly. Write it correctly on the line.

Spelling Words
Basic
so
go
no
me
where
who
what
when
why
how
Review
fast
lamp
jump
went

1. She gave em a gift.

_me_

2. eehWr is my map?

Where

3. ohW is your pal?

Who

4. neWh is the party?

When

5. Can you og fast?

_go_

6. woH will you do it?

How

Name _____

Phonics Review

- When there is only one vowel in a word and it is at the end, it usually stands for the long vowel sound. The words **me**, **so**, and **hi** all have long vowel sounds.

- You can add **'s** to a word to show that someone has or owns. Examples: This is the **dog's** dish. That is **Mom's** hat.

▶ Choose and write two words to complete each sentence.

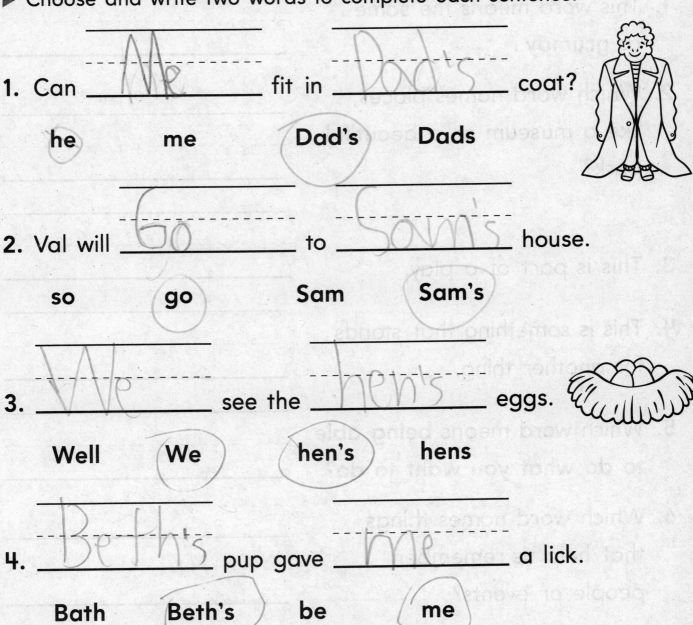

1. Can ___Me___ fit in ___Dad's___ coat?

    he   me   Dad's   Dads

2. Val will ___Go___ to ___Sam's___ house.

    so   go   Sam   Sam's

3. ___We___ see the ___hen's___ eggs.

    Well   We   hen's   hens

4. ___Beth's___ pup gave ___me___ a lick.

    Bath   Beth's   be   me

Power Words: Match

Word Bank

freedom   grouchy   monuments   scene   sights   symbol

▶ Write the Power Word from **Monument City** that best fits each item.

1. This word means the same as **grumpy**.

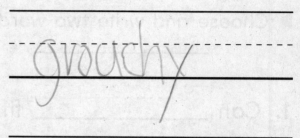

2. Which word names places, like a museum or a beautiful park?

3. This is part of a play.

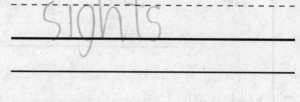

4. This is something that stands for another thing.

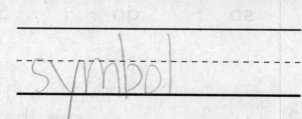

5. Which word means **being able to do what you want to do?**

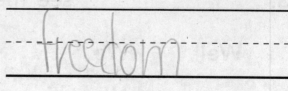

6. Which word names things that help us remember people or events?

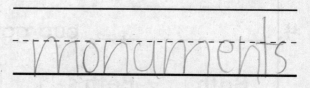

Name _____

Suffixes –y, –ful

A **suffix** is a word part that comes at the end of a base word. The **suffix –y** means "having or being like something." The **suffix –ful** means "full of." The **suffixes –y** and **–ful** change a base word to an adjective.

▶ Circle the words in the box that have the **suffix –y** or the **suffix –ful**. Then choose a word to complete each sentence. Use a dictionary to look up any words you do not know.

```
┌────────────(  Word Bank  )────────────┐
│                                        │
│  wind        windy       use    useful │
│                                        │
│  dirt        dirty       joy    joyful │
│                                        │
└────────────────────────────────────────┘
```

1. Boots are ___**useful**___ for keeping feet dry.

2. It was a very ___**windy**___ day.

3. The friends were ___**joyful**___ to see each other.

4. We can wash the ___**dirty**___ dishes.

Name _____

Elements of Drama

A **drama** is a story that is acted out by people. The **setting** of a drama is where and when it happens. The **cast of characters** is a list of characters, or the people or animals, in the drama. The **dialogue** is the words the characters say.

▶ Answer the questions about **Monument City**.

🔍 Pages 132–135 How do you know who the characters are? Where and when does the first scene take place?

_____

_____

_____

_____

🔍 Pages 136–137 How has the setting changed? What do Jeff's words tell you about him?

_____

_____

_____

Multiple-Meaning Words

A **multiple-meaning word** is a word that has more than one meaning. Look for clues in the text and pictures to help you figure out which meaning to use.

▶ Read the sentence. Then read both meanings of each underlined word. Put a check next to the meaning that best matches the underlined word.

1. We <u>saw</u> a bird make a nest in a tree.

a. a tool for cutting wood ☐

b. looked at something ☑

2. A cat makes a good <u>pet</u>.

a. an animal at home ☑

b. to pat gently ☐

3. We go to school in the <u>fall</u>.

a. the season after summer ☑

b. to go down quickly ☐

4. We walk our dog in the <u>park</u>.

a. open land for people to use ☑

b. to leave a car at a place ☐

Reference Sources

Use reference sources to find information.

- A **dictionary** lists many of the words in a language and their meanings in alphabetical order.

- A **glossary** is the part of a book that lists its important words and their meanings in alphabetical order.

- Many reference sources are also online.

▶ Put the words in alphabetical order. Then use a reference source to find their meanings. Write each word and its meaning to make a glossary!

| responsibility | globe | rights | citizen |

_____

- - - - - - - - - - - - - - - - - - - -

_____

- - - - - - - - - - - - - - - - - - - -

_____

- - - - - - - - - - - - - - - - - - - -

_____

- - - - - - - - - - - - - - - - - - - -

Name _____

_____

- -

_____

_____

- -

_____

_____

- -

_____

_____

- -

_____

_____

- -

_____

_____

- -

_____

_____

- -

_____

Name _____

Words to Know

▶ Write the word that best completes each sentence.

1. What __should__ we play today?

2. We __better__ make a mud cake.

3. What __shall__ do we need to make it?

4. Mom __gives__ us a pan to use.

5. We __began__ to put mud in the pan.

6. Making a mud cake is __always__ fun.

| Word Bank |
| always |
| began |
| better |
| gives |
| hurt |
| shall |
| should |
| things |

Name _____

Long *a* (VC*e*)

You can spell the **long a** sound with the **a-consonant-e** pattern, as in **plate**.

▶ Write each Basic Spelling Word in the correct column.

Words with long *a*		Words with short *a*
came	gave	map
make	shape	had
brave	plate	
late	flake	

Spelling Words

Basic

came

make

brave

late

gave

shape

plate

flake

map

had

Review

what

when

where

who

Name _____

Long *a* (VC*e*)

The word **ate** has a **vowel-consonant-e** pattern. The first vowel stands for the **long a** sound, and the final **e** is silent.

▶ Choose and write the word that names the picture.

___Word Bank___

| can | cane | snake | shapes |
| skates | gate | cake | shack |

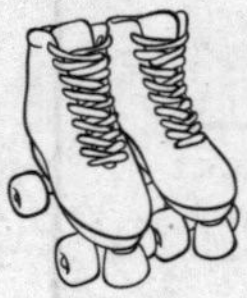

skates

cane

snake

shack

cake

shapes

Name _____

Long *a* (VC*e*)

You can spell the **long a** sound with the **a-consonant-e** pattern, as in **flake**.

▶ Read each word. Write the Basic Spelling Words that rhyme with it.

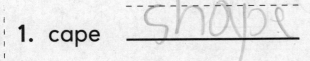

1. cape _____

2. game _____

3. date _____   _____

4. save _____   _____

5. bake _____   _____

▶ Which Basic Spelling Words did you **not** use? Circle them in the list. Then use each word in a sentence.

Spelling Words
Basic
came
make
brave
late
gave
shape
plate
flake
map
had
Review
what
when
where
who

Name _____

Power Words: Yes or No?

▶ Read each sentence. Circle **YES** if the word makes sense or **NO** if it does not. Rewrite the sentence so it makes sense.

Word Bank

contest

hope

liberty

1. I'll send my worst drawing to the art **contest**.

YES   (NO)

I'll send my best drawing to the art contest.

2. The Statue of **Liberty** stands for freedom.

(YES)   NO

3. I **hope** I lose a prize!

YES   (NO)

I hope I win a prize!

Name _____

Ideas and Support

When authors write to **persuade**, they try to get you to agree with an idea. They tell an **opinion**, or what they think or feel about something. Then authors give **reasons** for their opinion. Reasons can include facts, or things that can be proved.

▶ Answer the questions about **The Contest**.

🔍 Pages 164–165 What does Jade want you to think about the eagle? What reasons does she give to support her opinion?

_____

_____

_____

_____

_____

🔍 Pages 170–171 Which symbol does Lin think is the best? What reasons does Lin give to support her opinion?

_____

_____

_____

_____

_____

Name _____

Phonics Review

- When a word has a **vowel-consonant-e** pattern, the first vowel stands for a long sound, and the final **e** is silent. The word **cake** has the **long a** vowel sound.

- When the consonant **c** is followed by **e** or **i**, it stands for the /s/ sound. The words **face** and **cent** have the /s/ sound for the consonant **c**.

▶ Choose and write the word that answers each clue.

Word Bank
cent   flake   race   game   tape

1. This can help things stick. _tape_

2. You must run fast to win this. _race_

3. You can see this if it is very cold. _flake_

4. You can play this with a pal. _game_

5. You can spend this. _cent_

Module 6 · Week 2

Name _____

Suffixes –less, –ful

A **suffix** is a word part that comes at the end of a base word. The **suffix –less** means "without." The **suffix –ful** means "full of."

▶ Circle the words in the box that have the **suffix –less** or the **suffix –ful**. Then choose a word to complete each sentence. Use a dictionary to look up any words you do not know.

> **Word Bank**
>
> | spot | spotless | wonder | wonderful |
> | end | endless | peace | peaceful |

1. The park is _____wonderful_____ and calm.

2. We all did a _____peaceful_____ job today!

3. My sister and I keep our room _____spotless_____ .

4. The line into the movie seemed _____endless_____ .

Name _____

Power Words: Draw and Write

Word Bank

base   national   towers

▶ Draw a picture or write words that will help you remember each Power Word from **The Statue of Liberty**. Try to write more than you draw.

1. base

2. national

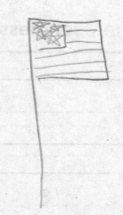

3. towers

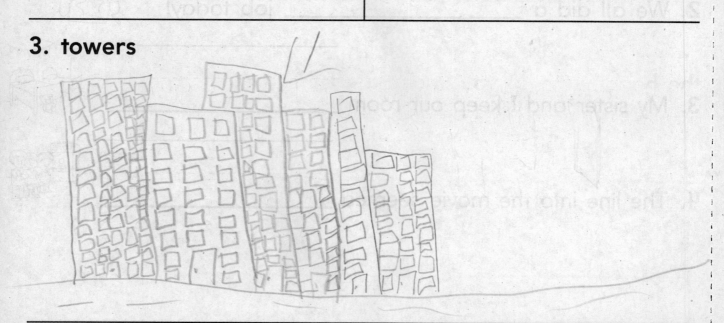

Name _____

Text Organization

Text organization is the way an author arranges information. Authors organize texts to go with their reason for writing. One way to organize informational text is **description**. In a description, an author tells **details** that describe what things are like one at a time. Sometimes authors include **headings** to tell what they are describing in each part of the text.

▶ Answer the questions about **The Statue of Liberty**.

🔍 Pages 184–186 Why did the author write this text? How does the way the text is organized help you?

_____

_____

_____

_____

🔍 Pages 190–192 What does this part tell about? How do the headings help you understand the text?

_____

_____

_____

_____

Name _____

Words to Know

carry	draw	eight	even
goes	may	seven	shows

▶ Circle the word that best completes each sentence.

1. I (carry, draw) my trucks in a bag.

2. I have (goes, seven) red trucks.

3. Here are my (eight, even) black trucks.

4. This red truck (goes, draw) very fast.

5. My pal Rick (shows, may) me his trucks.

6. Our trucks (carry, may) have a race.

Name _____

Long *i*, *o* (VC*e*)

You can spell the **long i** sound with the
i-consonant-e pattern, as in **bike**. You can
spell the **long o** sound with the **o-consonant-e**
pattern, as in **joke**.

▶ Write each Spelling Word in the correct column.

Words with long *i*	Words with long *o*
like	joke
white	stove
drive	home
time	poke
bike	
kite	

Spelling Words

Basic
like
white
drive
time
bike
kite
joke
stove
home
poke

Review
flake
late
shape
plate

Name _____

Long *i, o* (VC*e*)

When a word has a **vowel-consonant-e** pattern, the first vowel stands for a long sound, and the final **e** is silent. The word **nice** has a **long i** vowel sound. The word **hope** has a **long o** vowel sound.

▶ Choose and write the word that names the picture.

hole hop

hole

rob robe

robe

kit kite

kite

smell smile

smile

phone plane

phone

note not

note

smock smoke

smoke

bride bird

bride

Long *i*, *o* (VC*e*)

You can spell the **long i** sound with the **i-consonant-e** pattern, as in **like**. You can spell the **long o** sound with the **o-consonant-e** pattern, as in **stove**.

▶ Read each word. Follow the directions. Write the Spelling Word on the line.

Spelling Words			

Basic

like

white

drive

time

bike

kite

joke

stove

home

poke

Review

flake

late

shape

plate

1. **drove**   Change **o** to **i**.   *drive*

2. **kit**   Add an **e** after **t**.   *kite*

3. **lake**   Change **a** to **i**.   *like*

4. **bake**   Change **a** to **i**.   *bike*

5. **Jake**   Change **a** to **o**.   *Joke*

6. **Tim**   Add an **e** after **m**.   *Time*

Name _____

Power Words: Match

Word Bank

celebrate   Constitution   parade   share   tradition

▶ Write the Power Word from **Hooray for Holidays!** that best fits each item.

1. Which word means almost the same as **split** or **divide**?

   _____

2. This word names an important paper our leaders signed long ago.

   _____

3. Which word names a special thing people do year after year?

   _____

4. Which word describes a group of people marching?

   _____

5. This word tells what you do on a special day.

   _____

Name _____

Story Structure

Story structure is the way an author organizes a story.
In the beginning, the characters have a **problem**. The **events**
in the middle tell how the characters try to solve the problem.
At the end, the characters solve the problem in the **resolution**.

▶ Answer the questions about **Hooray for Holidays!**

🔍 Pages 204–207 What problem does Dave have?
How do the characters react to Dave's problem?

_____

_____

_____

_____

_____

🔍 Pages 208–210 How is the problem resolved? Why did the
author write this story the way she did?

_____

_____

_____

_____

_____

_____

Name _____

Phonics Review

- When a word has a **vowel-consonant-e** pattern, the first vowel stands for a long sound, and the final **e** is silent. The word **like** has a **long i** vowel sound. The word **note** has a **long o** vowel sound.

- Some words have other silent letters. The consonants **kn** stand for the /n/ sound in **knot**. The consonants **wr** stand for the /r/ sound in **write**.

▶ Choose and write the word that goes with each clue.

```
                    ( Word Bank )

    write        knock        ride        nose
```

1. You do this before you go into a pal's house.

   knock

2. You do this when you sit on a bike.

   ride

3. You can smell with this.

   nose

4. You can do this with a pen and pad.

   write

Name _____

Words About Actions

Action words tell what someone or something is doing.
Action words are called **verbs**.

▶ Read the story. Write an **action word** from the box to
complete each sentence. Use a dictionary to find the
meanings of any words you don't know.

> **Word Bank**
>
> mix   bake   wait   set   starts

My party _____ starts _____ soon. We still

need to _____ bake _____ a cake. Mom

and I _____ mix _____ the batter. We _____ set _____

it in the oven. Then we _____ wait _____ . It's done!
Now we can have fun!

Name _____

Words to Know

Knowing how to read and write these words can make you a better reader and writer.

```
┌─────────────────── Word Bank ───────────────────┐
│                                                  │
│   animal        heads        keep       Let's    │
│   point       something      voice      won't    │
│                                                  │
└──────────────────────────────────────────────────┘
```

▶ Write a word from the box to complete each sentence.

1. I tell Tom, "_____Let's_____ play in the grass."

2. I see _____something_____ in the grass.

3. I _____point_____ to it so Tom can see it, too.

4. What kind of _____animal_____ is this?

5. The animal _____heads_____ to the tree.

Name _____

Long *u*; VCe Pattern

You can spell the **long u** sound with the **u-consonant-e** pattern, as in **flute**. You can spell some long-vowel words by thinking about the **vowel-consonant-e (VCe)** pattern, as in **woke**.

▶ Write each Basic and Review Spelling Word in the correct column.

Words with long *u*	Words with long *a*	Words with long *i*	Words with long *o*
flute	woke	hike	woke
cute	bake	white	joke
Luke	game	drive	home
tube			
use			

Spelling Words

Basic

flute
cute
Luke
tube
use
woke
wake
hike
bake
game

Review

white
drive
joke
home

Name _____

Long *u*, *e* (VC*e*)

When a word has a **vowel-consonant-e** pattern, the first vowel stands for a long sound, and the final **e** is silent. The name **June** has a **long u** vowel sound. The name **Pete** has a **long e** vowel sound.

▶ Choose and write the word that names the picture.

tub   (tube)

tube

scent   (scene)

scene

(mute)   (mule)

mute

Eve   (Steve)

Steve

flat   (flute)

flute

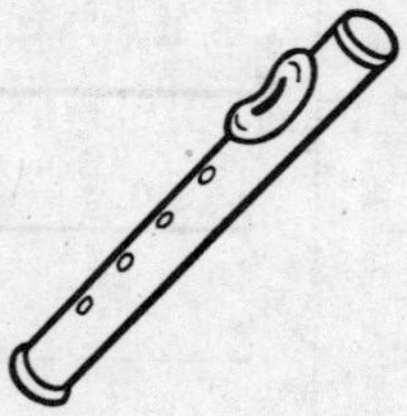

(cubes)   cubs

cubes

Name _____

Long *u*; VCe Pattern

You can spell the **long u** sound with the **u-consonant-e** pattern, as in **tube**. You can spell some long-vowel words by thinking about the **vowel-consonant-e (VCe) pattern**, as in **wake**.

▶ Write the Spelling Word that names each picture.

1.

game

2.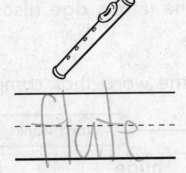

flute

3.

tube

4.

bake

5.

hike

6.

Luke

Name _____

Phonics Review

- When a word has a **vowel-consonant-e** pattern, the first vowel stands for a long sound, and the final **e** is silent. **Tune** has a **long u** vowel sound, and **these** has a **long e** vowel sound.

- When consonant **g** is followed by **e** or **i**, it often stands for the **j** sound. The words **gem** and **cage** have the **j** sound for consonant **g**. The letters **dge** also stand for the **j** sound, as in **badge**.

▶ Choose and write the word that completes the sentence.

> **Word Bank**
>
> cute   huge   judge   These

1. _____These_____ dogs are my pets.

2. The _____huge_____ black dog is Zeke.

3. The small _____cute_____ dog is Eve.

4. The _____judge_____ gave each pet a badge or prize.

Power Words: Match

Word Bank

mission   spectacular   break   problem   direction   landed

▶ Write the Power Word from **Sam & Dave Dig a Hole**
that best fits each item.

1. Which word tells what an
   airplane did at the end of
   a trip?

   _____

2. Which word names something
   that might make you worry?

   _____

3. Which word means the
   opposite of **dull** or **boring**?

   _____

4. This word tells something you
   might need if you're very tired.

   _____

5. Which word would you use to
   tell about important work?

   _____

6. People use this word when
   they describe which way to
   walk, such as left or right.

   _____

Name _____

Words About Feelings and Beliefs

Adjectives are words that describe people, places, or things.

- Some adjectives describe how a person **feels**.

- Some adjectives describe what a person **thinks** or **believes** about something.

▶ Write an **adjective** from the box to finish each sentence. Use a dictionary to find the meanings of any words you don't know.

Word Bank
great   afraid   proud   lonely   clever

1. Lou was _____ that he won the race.

2. My _____ sister solved the problem!

3. I was _____ to go into the dark cave.

4. That was a _____ movie!

5. The _____ puppy sat by itself.

Name _____

Point of View

When authors choose a **narrator** for a story, they decide how readers will experience the story. If a story is told from the first-person **point of view**, a character in the story is the narrator. The narrator uses the words **I**, **my**, or **me**. If a story is told from the third-person point of view, the narrator is not a character in the story. An outside narrator uses the words **he**, **she**, or **they**.

▶ Answer the questions about **Sam & Dave Dig a Hole.**

🔍 Pages 18–19 Is the narrator a character in the story? How do you know?

_____

- -

_____

- -

_____

🔍 Page 24 From which point of view is this story told? How do you know?

_____

- -

_____

- -

_____

Shades of Meaning

Synonyms are words that mean the same, or almost the same, thing. Small differences in the meanings of words are called **shades of meaning**.

▶ Read each group of synonyms. Then read the labels on the lines and write the words in order.

1. gobble   eat   nibble

slower ⟵—————————————⟶ faster

nibble   eat   gobble

2. toss   pitch   throw

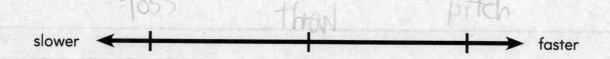

slower ⟵—————————————⟶ faster

toss   throw   pitch

3. giggle   roar   grin

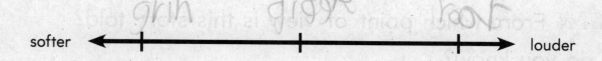

softer ⟵—————————————⟶ louder

grin   giggle   roar

4. amazing   great   super

good ⟵—————————————⟶ better

great   amazing   super

Name _____

Gather Information

You can make a **research plan** to gather information about a topic. First, **brainstorm** a list of questions to answer. Next, think of **sources** like books, websites, or people. When you have a list of sources, decide which ones will help you answer your questions. Then look for the answers!

▶ Look at the research plan below. Then answer the questions about it.

My Research Plan

Topic: Day and Night

Questions	Sources
What makes day change into night?	
Why does the moon change shape?	
How far away are the stars?	

Name _____

1. What is the topic of the research plan?

_____

- -

_____

2. Draw a line from each question in the research plan to the source you think will help you answer each question.

3. What is another question you could ask about day and night?

_____

- -

_____

- -

_____

4. What source could you use to answer your question?

_____

- -

_____

- -

_____

Name _____

Words to Know

▶ Write the word that best completes each sentence.

1. The egg is in the nest _____ the hen.

2. I _____ the egg crack.

3. Then the egg was _____ .

4. Now I _____ the little chick in my hand.

5. The chick is only one day _____ .

6. It will not go _____ from the hen.

Word Bank
below
far
hear
hold
old
only
open
round

Name _____

Long e Patterns

You can spell the **long e** sound with **e** as in **be**, with **ea** as in **team**, or **ee** as in **feet**.

▶ Write each Basic Spelling Word in the correct column.

Words with _e_	Words with _ea_	Words with _ee_
be	read	tree
tree	mean	keep
she	eat	see
		feet

Spelling Words

Basic

team
be
read
feet
tree
keep
eat
mean
see
she

Review

flute
tube
woke
game

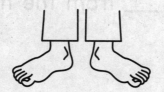

Name _____

Long e (ea, ee)

The word **eat** has the vowel team **ea**. The word **see** has the vowel team **ee**. The vowel teams **ea** and **ee** can stand for the **long e** sound.

▶ Choose and write the word that names the picture.

(wheel)   well

wheel

sheep   sheet

_____

teeth   treat

_____

sell   (seal)

_____

(peach)   patch

_____

tree   (three)

_____

Name _____

Long *e* Patterns

You can spell the **long e** sound with **e** as in **be**, with **ea** as in **team**, or **ee** as in **tree**.

▶ Read each sentence. Cross out the Spelling Word that is spelled incorrectly. Write it correctly on the line.

1. Can you se the show?

_____

2. Our teem won the game.

_____

3. My bare feat are cold.

_____

4. Lou likes to eet grapes.

_____

5. The bird lives in the tre.

_____

6. I reed books about dogs.

_____

Spelling Words
Basic
team
be
read
feet
tree
keep
eat
mean
see
she
Review
flute
tube
woke
game

Name _____

Power Words: Draw and Write

| dunes | shrubs | spines | rest |

▶ Draw a picture or write words that will help you remember each Power Word from **Deserts**. Try to write more than you draw.

1. dunes	2. shrubs
3. spines	4. rest

Name _____

Central Idea

The **topic** of an informational text is the person or thing it is about. The **central idea** is the main idea the author wants readers to know about the topic. Readers can use **supporting evidence** and **details** in a text to figure out the central idea.

▶ Answer the questions about **Deserts**.

🔍 Pages 40–41 What is this text about? What evidence helps you understand this?

_____

- -

_____

- -

_____

🔍 Pages 48–49 What does the author want you to learn? How do the photos and labels help you know?

_____

- -

_____

_____

- -

_____

_____

- -

_____

Name _____

Phonics Review

The vowel teams **ee** and **ea** can stand for the **long e** sound.
The vowel team **ea** can also stand for the **short e** sound in a
word. If you do not know a word, try the **long e** sound and
then the **short e** sound to see which makes sense.

▶ Choose and write a word to complete each sentence.
You will not use all the words!

Word Bank

thread   dream   heed   bread   leaves   head   three

1. Jean has a cap on her ___head___ .

2. When I am in a deep sleep, I ___dream___ .

3. I need ___thread___ to fix the hole in
my pants.

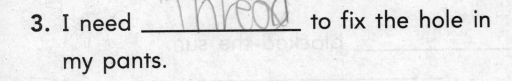

4. The ___leaves___ on the tree are green.

5. Do you like to eat jam and ___bread___ ?

Name _____

Suffix –less

A **suffix** is a word part that comes at the end of a **base word**. A suffix changes the meaning of the base word. The suffix **–less** means "without."

> **Word Bank**
>
> cloud   cloudless   end   endless

▶ Write a word from the box to finish each sentence. Use a dictionary to look up any words you do not know.

1. The long highway seemed ___endless___ !

2. You can see many stars on a ___cloudless___ night.

3. A big ___cloud___ blocked the sun.

4. We go home at the ___end___  of the day.

Name _____

Power Words: Yes or No?

▶ Read each sentence. Circle **YES** if the word makes sense or **NO** if it does not. Rewrite the sentence so it makes sense.

edges

trace

1. Blue flowers are growing along the **edges** of the road.

(YES)   NO

_____

- -

_____

- -

_____

2. I can use a ruler to **trace** my hand.

YES   (NO)

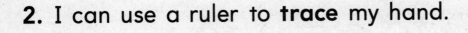

I can use a pensil to

trace my hand.

Name _____

Text Organization

Authors choose a **text organization**, or structure, to go with their reason for writing. **Chronological order** tells about events or steps to do something in order. Sequence words and graphic features can help readers know that a text is organized in chronological order. Look for the words **first**, **next**, and **last** or visuals, like numbers, as you read!

▶ Answer the questions about **Handmade**.

🔍 Pages 60–61 How does the author explain the steps? What clues help you know the text organization?

_____

- -

_____

_____

- -

_____

🔍 Pages 62–63 What does the author want you to learn? How does she organize the text?

_____

- -

_____

_____

- -

_____

Name _____

Words to Know

Word Bank

air	different	drink	enough
never	small	through	under

▶ Circle the word that best completes each sentence.

1. I want to (never, **drink**) some milk.

2. I take a (under, **small**) cup.

3. If I fill the cup, will that be (**enough**, different)?

4. I can walk with a full cup and (air, **never**) spill the milk.

5. I sit (**under**, through) a tree and drink my milk.

6. Now I want a (**different**, never) drink.

Name _____

Long *a* Vowel Teams

You can spell the **long a** sound with **ay**, as in **play**, or **ai**, as in **sail**.

▶ Write each Basic Spelling Word in the correct column.

Spelling Words

Basic

play

grain

sail

mail

may

rain

way

day

stay

pain

Review

see

read

mean

tree

Words with *ay*	Words with *ai*
play	sail
may	mail
way	grain
day	rain
stay	pain

Name _____

Long *a* (*ai, ay*)

The word **rain** has the vowel team **ai**. The word **day** has the vowel team **ay**. The vowel teams **ai** and **ay** can stand for the **long a** sound.

▶ Choose and write the word that names the picture.

(hay) hail		bread (braid)	
hay		_braid_	
(nails) mails		pant (paint)	
nails		_paint_	
track (tray)		(train) trace	
tray		_train_	
(rain) ran		chime (chain)	
rain		_chain_	

Name _____

Long *a* Vowel Teams

You can spell the **long a** sound with **ay**, as in **may**, or **ai**, as in **rain**.

▶ Write the missing letters. Then write the Spelling Word on the line.

Spelling Words

Basic

play

grain

sail

mail

may

rain

way

day

stay

pain

Review

see

read

mean

tree

1. gr__ai__n _____ grain

2. st__ay__ _____ stay

3. s__ai__l _____ sail

4. p__ai__n _____ pain

5. pl__ay__ _____ play

6. w__ay__ _____ way

Name _____

Power Words: Match

> **Word Bank**

| popular | fossils | rim | hike | affect |

▶ Write the Power Word from **Grand Canyon** that best fits each item.

1. Which word names what you might do on a trail?

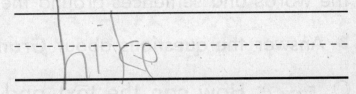

hike

2. Which word describes things that many people like?

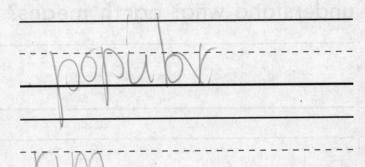

popular

3. This word means almost the same as **edge**.

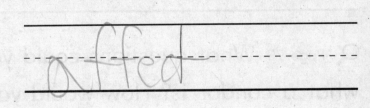

rim

4. This word means **to change in some way**.

affect

5. This word names parts of very old plants and animals found inside rocks.

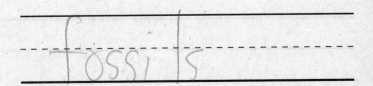

fossils

Name _____

Content-Area Words

Some informational texts have special words about science or social studies topics. Ask yourself questions about words you do not know. Then use **context clues** to figure out the meaning of the words. Context clues can be text features such as titles, headings, pictures, or photographs. They can also be the words and sentences around the word you do not know.

▶ Answer the questions about **Grand Canyon.**

🔍 Page 75 How can the text and photo help you understand what **earth** means?

_____

- - - - - - - - - - - - - - - - - - - -

_____

- - - - - - - - - - - - - - - - - - - -

_____

🔍 Page 79 What questions could you ask to figure out what a condor is? How would you answer them?

_____

- - - - - - - - - - - - - - - - - - - -

_____

- - - - - - - - - - - - - - - - - - - -

_____

Phonics Review

The vowel teams **ai** and **ay** can stand for the **long a** sound.

▶ Choose and write the word that completes the sentence.

1. I get wet in the __*rain*__ .

    ran   (**rain**)   **ray**

2. You can __*stay*__ here with me.

    say   **stain**   (**stay**)

A **contraction** is a shorter way of saying two words together. To make a contraction, an apostrophe (') takes the place of one or more letters. Examples of contractions: **hasn't = has not, we'll = we will, he's = he is, I'm = I am.**

▶ Combine the underlined words to write each contraction.

3. <u>She is</u> my pal.   *she's*

4. Jake <u>did not</u> go with me.   *didn't*

5. <u>I will</u> play in the sand.   *I'll*

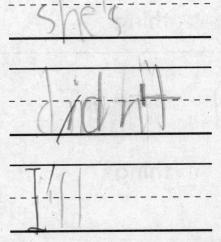

Name _____

Words About Places and Things

Nouns are words that name people, places, or things.

- Nouns that name places tell **where** something is happening.

- Nouns that name things tell **what** something is.

▶ Write a **noun** from the box to match each picture. Then draw a circle to tell if the word names a place or a thing. Use a dictionary to find the meanings of words you don't know.

> ### Places and Things
>
> cave   leaf   desert   woods   bug   shell

1. _bug_

place   (thing)

2. _cave_

(place)   thing

3. _desert_

(place)   thing

4. _leaf_

place   (thing)

5. _shell_

place   (thing)

6. _woods_

(place)   thing

Name _____

Words to Know

Knowing how to read and write these words can make you a better reader and writer.

> **Word Bank**
>
> along   answer   children   going
>
> mother   talk   upon   woman

▶ Circle the word that best completes each sentence.

1. Is your (mother, children) at work?

2. The cat sits (upon, along) the bed.

3. Joe is (answer, going) out.

4. Will you come (along, upon) with me?

5. I know the right (talk, answer).

6. We will (going, talk) to Mom today.

7. The (children, answer) play tag.

8. Who is that (woman, talk) in the hat?

Name _____

Long o

You can spell the **long o** sound with **ow**, as in **snow**, and **oa**, as in **road**.

▶ Write each Spelling Word in the correct column.

Words with *ow*	Words with *oa*
show	boat
row	coat
grow	road
low	toad
blow	
snow	

Name _____

Long o (oa, ow)

The vowel teams **oa** and **ow** can stand for the **long o** sound.

▶ Read the word. Circle the picture that matches the word. Then write the letters that stand for the **long o** sound.

1. goat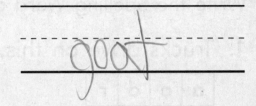

2. bowl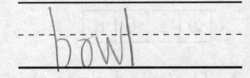

3. goal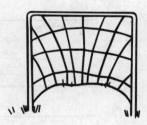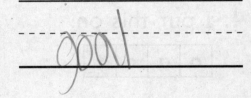

4. crow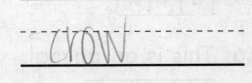

Name _____

Long *o*

You can spell the **long o** sound with **ow**, as in **show**, and **oa**, as in **boat**.

▶ Read each clue. Unscramble the word.
Write the Spelling Word correctly on the line.

1. Trucks drive on this.

| a | o | d | r |

_____

2. I see this in winter.

| w | s | o | n |

_____

3. The wind does this.

| w | b | o | l |

_____

4. I put this on.

| o | a | c | t |

_____

5. This is not high.

| o | l | w |

_____

6. This is an animal.

| a | o | d | t |

_____

▶ Choose other Spelling Words. Make up a clue for each one. Scramble the letters. Ask a partner to write the words correctly.

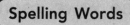

Spelling Words

Basic

show

row

grow

low

blow

snow

boat

coat

road

toad

Review

play

grain

mail

stay

Name _____

Phonics Review

The vowel teams **oa**, **ow**, and **oe** can all stand for the **long o** sound. The vowel team **ie** can stand for the **long i** sound.

▶ Write two words to complete each sentence.

1. ___Joe___ bumped his ___toe___ .

(Joe)   (toe)   goal   low

2. I can ___show___ you how to ___tie___ a bow.

(show)   pie   grow   (tie)

3. The ___boat___ can ___float___ on the lake.

flat   (boat)   (float)   road

4. Dad ___knows___ how to bake a ___pie___ .

hoe   (knows)   pine   (pie)

5. Grab a ___coat___ to go in the ___snow___ .

cot   (coat)   low   (snow)

Name _____

Power Words: Match

interrupt   follow   involved   supposed   relaxing   warn

▶ Write the Power Word from **Interrupting Chicken**
that best fits each item.

1. Which word do you use if
   something bad may happen?   _____

2. This word means that you
   have to do something.   _____

3. Which word means to walk
   behind someone?   _____

4. Which word tells what you
   are doing when you rest?   _____

5. Which word means to talk
   while another person talks?   _____

6. This word means to be a
   part of something.   _____

Name _____

Words About Actions and Directions

Action words, or **verbs**, tell what someone or something is doing. **Direction words** tell where a person or thing is going.

▶ Write one action and one direction word to finish each sentence about the picture. Use a dictionary to find the meanings of any words you don't know.

Word Bank

Action Words		Direction Words	
run	swim	up	through
dig	fly	down	across

1. Birds ___fly___ ___across___ the sky.

2. Squirrels ___run___ ___up___ a tree.

3. Rabbits ___dig___ ___down___ into the ground.

4. Turtles ___swim___ ___through___ the water.

Name _____

Characters

A **character** is the person, animal, or thing a story is about. Understanding what a character is like can help readers understand and describe the **reasons** for their **actions**.

▶ Answer the questions about **Interrupting Chicken.**

🔍 Pages 118–119 How does Papa feel when Chicken keeps interrupting? How do you know?

_____

- -

_____

- -

_____

🔍 Pages 124–125 What is Chicken like? Why does she keep interrupting?

_____

- -

_____

- -

_____

Name _____

Classify and Categorize

To **classify** words, sort the words into a group. To **categorize** words, name the group or tell how the words are alike.

▶ Read the words in the box. How can you sort them in three groups? Underline the words in one group. Circle the words in another group. Draw a square around the words in a third group.

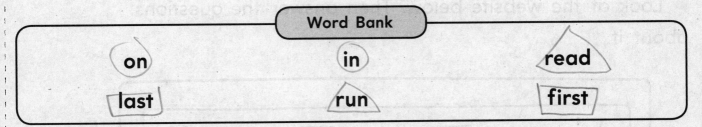

Word Bank

on   in   read

last   run   first

▶ Pick one word from each group. Write what it means on the lines below.

1. _____last_____

_____

2. _____

_____

3. _____

Name _____

Digital Texts and Features

- **Digital tools** are types of technology used for research or to give information.

- **Digital texts** are read or experienced through digital tools.

- **Digital features** can help you find information. A **menu** has links to other pages. An **icon** is a picture that stands for something.

▶ Look at the website below. Then answer the questions about it.

Name _____

1. What is the title of the website?

Lions

2. What would you tap on if you wanted to find
out information about tigers?

click on the word tiger

3. Where would you look if you wanted to find
out more information about lions?

click on the other tabs

4. What would you tap on if you wanted to
find some videos of lions?

click on the icon of the video

Name _____

Words to Know

Word Bank

bring	eyes	family	girl
move	soon	together	warm

▶ Write a word from the box to complete each sentence.

1. Eve and I play _____together_____ in the park.

2. Did you _____bring_____ a ball, Eve?

3. It is very _____warm_____ out!

4. We soon _____move_____ into some shade.

▶ Write a word from the box for each picture.

5.

_____girl_____

6.

_____eyes_____

7.

_____family_____

Name _____

Long *i* Patterns

You can spell the **long i** sound with **y**, as in **sky**, **ie**, as in **pie**, and **igh**, as in **night**.

▶ Write each Spelling Word in the correct column.

Words with y	Words with ie	Words with igh
my	pie	night
try	tie	light
sky		
fly		
by		
dry		

Name _____

Long *i* (*igh*, *y*)

The letters **igh** stand for the **long i** sound. The letter **y** sometimes stands for the **long i** sound at the end of word or syllable.

▶ Write the correct word to complete each sentence.

1. The light from the sun is _____ .

   bay   **bright**   **by**

2. You can do it if you _____ .

   tie   **tight**   **try**

3. The bird is _____ in the sky.

   hive   **high**   **hay**

4. I will help _____ the dishes.

   dry   **did**   **drive**

5. A coat that is too small is _____ .

   tin   **time**   **tight**

Spelling

Long *i* Patterns

You can spell the **long i** sound with **y**, as in **sky**, **ie**, as in **pie**, and **igh**, as in **night**.

▶ Write the Spelling Word that names each picture.

Spelling Words

Basic

my
try
sky
fly
by
dry
pie
tie
night
light

Review

show
grow
blow
snow

1.

_____

2.

_____

3.

_____

4.

_____

5.

_____

6.

_____

▶ Which four Basic Spelling Words did you **not** use?
Circle them in the list. Write a sentence for each word.

Name _____

Power Words: Draw and Write

Word Bank

storyteller	sly	boldly

▶ Draw a picture or write words that will help you remember each Power Word from **Little Red Riding Hood**. Try to write more than you draw.

1. storyteller

2. sly

3. boldly

Name _____

Elements of Drama

A **drama** is a story that is acted out by people. The **setting** tells where and when the drama takes place. The **cast of characters** is the list of characters, or who is in the drama. The **dialogue** is the words that the characters speak.

▶ Answer the questions about **Little Red Riding Hood**.

🔍 Pages 140–141 How do you know who the characters in this drama are? Where does this drama take place?

_____

_ _

_____

_ _

_____

🔍 Pages 146–147 Who is talking on these pages? What do the words that Coyote says help you learn about him?

_____

_ _

_____

_ _

_____

_ _

_____

Name _____

Phonics Review

The spelling patterns **igh** and **y** can stand for the **long i** sound. Sometimes, the letters **i** and **o** have a long vowel sound when they are closed by consonants. Try both sounds to see which makes sense.

▶ Write the word that names the picture.

1.

   chick   child   chill   _____

2.

   fly   fill   flip   _____

3.

   name   night   nine   _____

4.

   got   gold   goat   _____

5.

   blinks   bikes   blinds   _____

Name _____

Suffix –ly

A **suffix** is a word part that comes at the end of a base word. The **suffix –ly** tells how or when something is done. It changes a word into an adverb.

▶ Write a word to finish each sentence. Use a dictionary to look up any words you do not know.

> **Word Bank**
>
> nice   nicely   brave   bravely

1. John does ____nice____ things for his friends.

2. Ana stood ____bravely____ in front of the class.

3. Patrick is ____brave____ because he tries new foods.

4. Clara painted ____nicely____ during art class.

Name _____

Power Words: Yes or No?

▶ Read each sentence. Circle **YES** if the word makes sense or **NO** if it does not. Rewrite the sentence so it makes sense.

1. Winter comes before **autumn**.

YES   NO

_____

- -

_____

2. "That was fun!" she **chirped**.

YES   NO

_____

- -

_____

3. When I **labor**, I am playing.

YES   NO

_____

- -

_____

Name _____

Setting

The **setting** of a story is where and when the story takes place. Readers can use the **details** and evidence from the words and pictures of a story to **describe** what the setting is.

▶ Answer the questions about **The Grasshopper & the Ants.**

🔍 Pages 166–169 What time of year is it in this part of the story? How have the woods changed?

_____

- -

_____

- -

_____

🔍 Page 170 What are the woods like now? How has the setting changed?

_____

- -

_____

- -

_____

Name _____

Words to Know

┌─────────────── **Word Bank** ───────────────┐

| brown | few | funny | myself |
| new | once | thank | words |

└──┘

▶ Read the clues. Write the word from the Word Bank that goes with each clue.

1. You speak using these. _____

2. A tree trunk could be this. _____

3. A joke should be this. _____

4. This is not old. _____

5. This is not many. _____

6. This means one time. _____

Name _____

r-Controlled Vowel *ar*

You can spell the /är/ sound with **ar**, as in **barn**.

▶ Write each Spelling Word in the correct box.

Words with *ar*

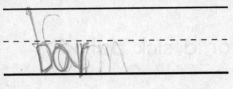
barn

yarn

Words with *ard*

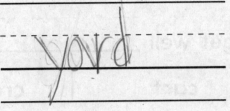
yard

Words with *arm*

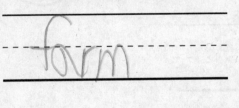
farm

arm

Words with *arn*

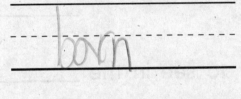
barn

yarn

Other words with *ar*

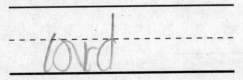
card

bark

Name _____

r-Controlled Vowel *ar*

The letter **r** can control a vowel sound and change it. The letters **ar** stand for the vowel sound in **car**.

▶ Write the correct word to complete each sentence.

1. Tim made a get well __card__ for a sick pal.

   (card)   cart   crab

2. It can be __hard__ to ride a bike.

   had   (hard)   harm

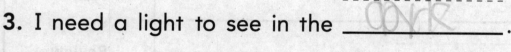

3. I need a light to see in the __dark__.

   damp   drove   dark

4. Gram will knit me a hat and a __scarf__.

   start   scarf   skip

5. We will plant the tree in the __yard__.

   yard   yell   yarn

Name _____

r-Controlled Vowel *ar*

You can spell the /är/ sound with **ar**, as in **farm**.

▶ Read each word. Write the Basic Spelling Words that rhyme with it.

1. cart art _____

2. lark bark _____

3. hard card yard

4. darn yarn barn

5. car bar jar

6. harm farm arm

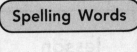

Spelling Words

Basic

farm
arm
yard
art
jar
bar
barn
bark
card
yarn

Review

try
dry
night
pie

▶ What other words rhyme with this week's Spelling Words? Make a list on another sheet of paper.

231

Name _____

Power Words: Match

Word Bank

lesson   wise   tale   nonsense   reply

▶ Write the Power Word from **Thank You, Mr. Aesop**
that best fits each item.

1. Which word means almost
   the same as **silly**?   _____

2. This word means something
   that you learn.   _____

3. Which word means
   something you say as an
   answer to a question?   _____

4. This word means almost
   the same as **story**.   _____

5. Which word means almost
   the same as **smart**?   _____

Name _____

Central Idea

The **topic** of an informational text is the person or thing it tells about. The **central idea**, or main idea, is what the author wants readers to take away from reading the text.

▶ Answer the questions about **Thank You, Mr. Aesop.**

🔍 Pages 194–195 Who is this text mostly about? What does the author tell you about Aesop?

_____

- -

_____

_____

- -

_____

🔍 Page 198 What does the author want you to learn from this text? What evidence lets you know?

_____

- -

_____

_____

- -

_____

_____

- -

_____

Name _____

Phonics Review

The letters **ar** stand for the vowel sound in **car**.
Every syllable has a vowel sound. Break a long word
into syllables to read it. First find the vowel spellings.
Then divide between the two consonants.

| car / pet |
| VC / CV |

▶ Write a word from the box to name each picture.

```
          Word Bank
shark   cactus   barn   kitten   yarn   magnet
```

1. cactus

2. barn

3. shark

4. cat

5. yarn

6. magnet

Name _____

Suffix –*ly*

A **suffix** is a word part that comes at the end of a base word. The **suffix –ly** tells how or when something is done. It changes a word into an adverb.

▶ Choose the word that best completes each sentence. Write the word on the line. Look up any base words you do not know in the dictionary.

1. I sang _____ to myself.

   soft   **softly**

2. The girl looked _____ at her broken toy.

   sad   **sadly**

3. Sara _____ watches TV.

   rare   **rarely**

4. Gloves keep your hands _____.

   warm   **warmly**

Name _____

Words to Know

Learn these words. You will see them in your reading
and use them in your writing.

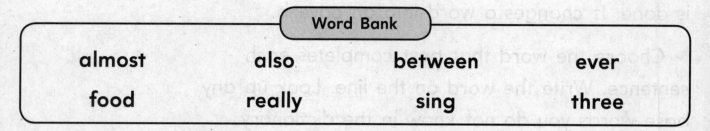

Word Bank

| almost | also | between | ever |
| food | really | sing | three |

▶ Write a word from the box to complete each sentence.

1. It is _____ time to eat.

2. All the _____ looks good.

3. I sit _____ Mom and Dad.

4. I pass out _____ cups.

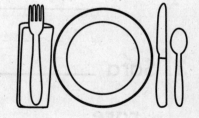

5. I _____ set out three plates.

6. This will be the best meal _____!

Name _____

r-Controlled Vowels *or, ore*

Spell the /ôr/ sound with **or**, as in **horn**, or with **ore** (a trigraph) at the end of a word, as in **more**.

▶ Write each Spelling Word in the correct column.

Words with *or*	Words with *ore*
_____	_____
_____	_____
_____	_____
_____	_____
_____	_____
_____	_____
_____	_____
_____	_____

Spelling Words

Basic

horn

fork

corn

short

born

door

more

shore

story

score

Review

barn

jar

art

yarn

237

Name _____

r-Controlled Vowels *or, ore*

The letters **or** and **ore** stand for the same **r**-controlled vowel sound. The letters **or** stand for the vowel sound in **for**. The letters **ore** stand for the same vowel sound in **more**.

▶ Choose and write a word to complete each sentence.

_____

- - - - - - - - - - - - - - - - -

1. I put the _____ by the plate.

   form   **fork**   **farm**

_____

- - - - - - - - - - - - - - - - -

2. Jan _____ a coat to play in the snow.

   worn   **warm**   **wore**

_____

- - - - - - - - - - - - - - - - -

3. Mark has a _____ on his bike.

   horn   **horse**   **harm**

_____

- - - - - - - - - - - - - - - - -

4. The _____ of the game is five to five.

   scar   **shore**   **score**

_____

- - - - - - - - - - - - - - - - -

5. A _____ has long legs.

   storm   **store**   **stork**

Name _____

r-Controlled Vowels *or*, *ore*

Spell the /ôr/ sound with **or**, as in **fork**, or with **ore** (a trigraph) at the end of a word, as in **shore**.

▶ Read each word. Write the Spelling Words that rhyme with it and have the same spelling pattern.

1. pork _____

_____

2. glory _____

3. fort _____   _____

4. torn _____   _____

_____

5. core _____   _____

_____

Spelling Words
Basic
horn
fork
corn
short
born
door
more
shore
story
score
Review
barn
jar
art
yarn

Phonics Review

The letters **ar** stand for the vowel sound in **car**. The letters **or** and **ore** stand for the vowel sound in **for** and **more**.

Every syllable has a vowel sound. You can break a long word into syllables to read it. First, find the vowel spellings. Then, divide between the two consonants. Blend each syllable, and then put them together.

for / get
VC   CV

▶ Choose and write a word to name each picture.

Word Bank

garden   hornet   carpet   harness

1. _____

2. _____

3. _____

4. _____

Name _____

Power Words: Match

| terrific | ingredients | nutrients | soil | sow | harvest |

▶ Write the Power Word from **So You Want to Grow a Taco?** that best fits each item.

1. Which word tells how to plant seeds?

_____

2. Which word means the opposite of **awful**?

_____

3. This word tells what farmers do when their corn is ripe.

_____

4. This word names the things you need to make a food like soup.

_____

5. Which word means the same as **dirt**?

_____

6. This word tells what vitamins are.

_____

Name _____

Words About Places and Things

A **noun** that names a place tells **where** something happens.

A **noun** that names a thing tells **what** something is.

▶ Choose a noun from the box to complete each sentence. Then draw a circle to tell whether the noun names a **place** or **thing**. Use a dictionary to find the meanings of any words you don't know.

Word Bank			
city	truck	store	kite

_____

1. We buy food at the _____ .

   place   **thing**

2. I can fly a _____ .

   place   **thing**

3. My dad drives a _____ .

   place   **thing**

Name _____

Text Organization

Authors choose a **text organization**, or structure, to fit their reason for writing. **Chronological order** tells about events in order. It also tells how to make or do something in order. Authors use clue words, like **first**, **next**, and **last**, to tell readers the steps to follow. Sometimes they use graphic features, like numbered steps.

▶ Answer the questions about **So You Want to Grow a Taco?**

🔍 Pages 20 and 22 How does the author explain how to grow corn? What clues help you know?

_____

_____

_____

_____

🔍 Pages 28–29 What does the author want you to learn here? How does she organize the information?

_____

_____

_____

_____

Reference Sources

You can find the meaning of a word you don't know in a **dictionary** or **glossary**. The words in these sources are listed in **ABC order**. This order is the same as the letters in the alphabet.

▶ Write each group of words in ABC order. Then choose one word. Look up the word in a dictionary and write its meaning.

1. leaf, hot, shout

_____   _____   _____

_____   _____   _____

2. bug, bread, dig

_____   _____   _____

_____   _____   _____

_____

Word: _____

_____

Meaning: _____

_____

_____

Name _____

Nonfiction Forms

Nonfiction texts can be found in many things you read: **books**, **newspapers**, and even **magazines**. Get to know their parts so you can use them to find information.

- **Table of contents:** tells what page each thing is on
- **Article:** piece of writing in a newspaper or magazine
- **Recipe:** instructions for cooking food
- **Letter:** message written to someone
- **Text feature:** part of a text, such as captions, headings, headlines, and lists, that call out something important
- **Graphic feature:** a visual, like a photo, illustration, or chart, that gives information

▶ Look at the newspaper article below. Then answer the questions about it.

Community Garden a Big Hit

The community garden opened this week. Dozens of neighbors came to the opening party. The garden is the first one in our town. But if the excitement continues, the mayor says he will consider opening more.

Neighbors got started planting right away.

Name _____

1. What information does the headline give?

_____

_____

2. Why does the author include a photo?

_____

_____

3. What information does the caption give readers?

_____

_____

4. What information can you find in a table of contents?

_____

_____

_____

Name _____

Words to Know

▶ Write the word that best completes each sentence.

_____

1. Max is the _____ with the red hat.

_____

2. His _____ is the man next to him.

_____

3. They walk through the _____
together.

_____

4. Max _____ "Hi" to his pal Tim.

_____

5. Tim _____ "HELLO!" to Max
when he saw him.

_____

6. _____ they will all sit together.

Word Bank
boy
door
father
Maybe
nearest
says
shouted
until

▶ Write a sentence for a word you did not write yet.

_____

_____

_____

Name _____

r-Controlled Vowels *er*, *ir*, *ur*

You can spell the /ûr/ sound with **er**, as in **fern**, with **ir**, as in **girl**, or with **ur**, as in **fur**.

▶ Write each Spelling Word in the correct column.

Words with er	Words with ir	Words with ur

Name _____

r-Controlled Vowels *er*, *ir*, *ur*

The **r**-controlled vowels **er**, **ir**, and **ur** stand for the same vowel sound. The words **her**, **sir**, and **fur** have the same **r**-controlled vowel sound but different spellings.

▶ Choose and write a word to name each picture.

1. herd   hard   here

_____

- - - - - - - - - - - - - - - - - - - -

_____

2. short   shirt   skirt

_____

- - - - - - - - - - - - - - - - - - - -

_____

3. curls   cubs   car

_____

- - - - - - - - - - - - - - - - - - - -

_____

4. bored   bird   braid

_____

- - - - - - - - - - - - - - - - - - - -

_____

5. farm   form   fern

_____

- - - - - - - - - - - - - - - - - - - -

_____

Name _____

r-Controlled Vowels er, ir, ur

You can spell the /ûr/ sound with **er**, as in **her**, with **ir**, as in **sir**, or with **ur**, as in **hurt**.

▶ Read each sentence. Cross out the Spelling Word that is spelled incorrectly. Write it correctly on the line.

1. The furn grows by the tree.

   _____

2. It is my tirn at bat.

   _____

3. That gurl is my friend.

   _____

4. My cat has soft fer.

   _____

5. The boy is in therd grade.

   _____

6. An eagle is a berd.

   _____

Spelling Words
Basic
her
fern
girl
sir
stir
bird
fur
hurt
turn
third
Review
horn
fork
story
score

Name _____

Power Words: Draw and Write

Word Bank

sturdy	cook

▶ Draw a picture or write words that will help you remember each Power Word from **Which Part Do We Eat?** Try to write more than you draw.

1. sturdy

2. cook

Name _____

Elements of Poetry

Poets use words in different ways to make their poems more interesting and fun to read. **Rhythm** is the beat you hear in poems and music. **Repetition** is when the same words or sounds appear over and over again. Repetition adds to a poem's rhythm. Words that **rhyme** have the same sound or sounds at the end. Rhyming words make a **pattern** of repeating sounds.

▶ Answer the questions about **Which Part Do We Eat?**

🔍 Pages 42–43 What rhythm and rhyme do you hear?

_____

_____

_____

_____

🔍 Pages 44–45 Which words does the author repeat? Why?

_____

_____

_____

Name _____

Phonics Review

The **r**-controlled vowels **er**, **ir**, and **ur** stand for the same sound, as in the words **verb**, **dirt**, and **curb**.

Every syllable has a vowel sound. Break a long word into syllables to read it. First, find the vowel spellings. Then, divide between the two consonants.

▶ Choose and write a word to complete each sentence.

_____

1. A _____ likes to ride the waves.

   surfer   suburb   supper

   _____

2. Put the dirty shirt in the _____ .

   hunger   hammer   hamper

   _____

3. I saw animal acts at the _____ .

   cellar   circus   chatter

   _____

4. Mom put hot soup in the _____ .

   temper   third   thermos

Name _____

Prefix *un–*

A **prefix** is a word part that comes at the beginning of a **base word**. A prefix changes the meaning of the word. The **prefix un–** can mean "not" or "opposite of."

▶ Use a word from the box with the **prefix un–** to complete each sentence. Use a dictionary to look up any words you do not know.

Word Bank

| unhurt | unlock | unzip | untie |
---

1. He used a key to _____ the front door.

2. I can _____ my jacket if I get too warm.

3. Please _____ the bow.

4. Jen was _____ after she fell.

Name _____

Power Words: Yes or No?

pounding	smooth	delicious	stretched

▶ Read each sentence. Circle **YES** if the word makes sense or **NO** if it does not. Rewrite the sentence so it makes sense.

1. The rain is **pounding** in the house.

       YES   NO

_____

- -

_____

2. He **stretched** his **smooth** socks over his feet.

       YES   NO

_____

- -

_____

3. Most people think rocks are **delicious**.

       YES   NO

_____

- -

_____

Name _____

Story Structure

Story structure is the way an author organizes the **events** in a story to make it fun to read. The beginning of the story usually explains the **problem**. The events in the middle tell how the characters try to solve the problem. The end explains the **resolution**, or how the problem is solved. These events make up the story's **plot**.

▶ Answer the questions about **The Talking Vegetables**.

🔍 Pages 58–59 What is the problem and how do the characters react to it?

_____

_____

_____

_____

🔍 Pages 72–75 How was the problem resolved? How does the story's structure make it fun to read?

_____

_____

_____

_____

Name _____

Words to Know

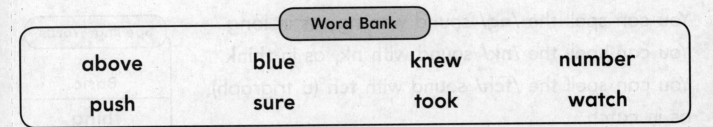

Word Bank

above	blue	knew	number
push	sure	took	watch

▶ Circle the word that best completes each sentence.

1. My dad (took, watch) us to the beach.

2. We sit on a (blue, sure) mat.

3. I (push, watch) a bird fly by.

4. It goes (knew, above) my head.

5. I (push, took) at the sand with my feet.

6. I (number, knew) this would be a fun day.

Name _____

Final Blends; Inflections –s, –es

You can spell the /ng/ sound with **ng**, as in **long**.
You can spell the /nk/ sound with **nk**, as in **think**.
You can spell the /tch/ sound with **tch** (a trigraph), as in **catch**.

You can add **–s** or **–es** to make words plural, as in **cents** and **catches**.

▶ Write each Spelling Word in the correct box.
You will use some words two times.

Words with **ng**	Words with **nk**	Words with **tch** at the end
_____	_____	_____
-------------	-------------	-------------
_____	_____	_____
-------------	-------------	-------------
_____	_____	_____

Word pairs with –s or –es

-------------	-------------	-------------
_____	_____	_____
_____	_____	_____
-------------	-------------	-------------
_____	_____	_____

Spelling Words

Basic

thing

think

long

thank

pitch

pitches

cent

cents

catch

catches

Review

third

turn

her

stir

Name _____

Final Blends *ng*, *nk*; Inflection *–ing*

The consonant blends **ng** and **nk** blend so closely together, they make new sounds. The letters **ng** stand for the last sound in **thing**. The letters **nk** stand for the last sound in **think**.

▶ Choose and write a word to name each picture.

bank   bang

_____

_____

swung   swing

_____

_____

rink   ring

_____

_____

sink   sing

_____

_____

The **–ing ending** tells that an action is happening now.

▶ Write a sentence about something that is happening now. Use one of these words: **feeling**, **reading**, **thinking**.

_____

_____

_____

Name _____

Final Blends; Inflections –s, –es

You can spell the /ng/ sound with **ng**, as in **thing**.
You can spell the /nk/ sound with **nk**, as in **thank**.
You can spell the /tch/ sound with **tch** (a trigraph), as in **catch**.

You can add **–s** or **–es** to make words plural, as in **cents** and **catches**.

▶ Write the Spelling Word that best completes each sentence.

_____

1. Say _____ you for his help.

_____

2. I will _____ a ball, and

_____

   you _____ it.

_____

3. When you take a test, _____ hard.

_____

4. Mia waited a _____ time.

_____

5. Four _____ are in my bank.

Spelling Words
Basic
thing
think
long
thank
pitch
pitches
cent
cents
catch
catches
Review
third
turn
her
stir

Name _____

Power Words: Match

Word Bank

indigo	wonder	syrup	juicy	ripe

▶ Write the Power Word from **Yum! ¡MmMm! ¡Qué rico!** that best fits each item.

1. This means that fruit or vegetables are ready to pick and eat.

   _____

   _____

   _____

2. Which word names the color of blueberries?

   _____

   _____

3. Which word means the opposite of **dry**?

   _____

   _____

4. This word names something thick and sweet that you can pour.

   _____

   _____

5. Which word could you use to tell about something that is really amazing?

   _____

   _____

Name _____

Elements of Poetry

Poets use words in special ways to make their poems interesting and fun to read. **Describing words** help readers create a picture in their minds about how things look, sound, feel, smell, and taste. **Rhythm** is the beat that you hear in poems and music. **Alliteration** is the repetition of words that have the same sound or sounds at the beginning. These repeating sounds make a **pattern**.

▶ Answer the questions about **Yum! ¡MmMm! ¡Qué rico!**

🔍 Page 88 What is being described in this poem? What do you picture in your mind?

_____
- -
_____
- -

🔍 Page 90 What pattern of sounds do you hear? How does it make the poem more fun to read?

_____
- -
_____
- -

Name _____

Phonics Review

The final blend **ng** stands for the last sound in **wing**. The final blend **nk** stands for the last sound in **wink**.

▶ Write **sink** and **ring** to complete the sentence.

_____   _____

- - - - - - - - - - - - -   - - - - - - - - - - - - -

Don't drop the _____ in the _____ .

The **endings –ing**, **–s**, and **–es** can tell when an action happens. The **endings –s** and **–es** can also mean "more than one" of something.

▶ Choose and write a word to complete each sentence. Use the words from the box.

_____

- - - - - - - - - - - - - - - - -

1. Two _____ are playing.

_____

- - - - - - - - - - - - - - - - -

2. One fox _____ bugs.

_____

- - - - - - - - - - - - - - - - -

3. One fox _____ a hole.

_____

- - - - - - - - - - - - - - - - -

4. Now the foxes are _____ .

> **Word Bank**
>
> catches
>
> digs
>
> foxes
>
> sleeping

Name _____

Prefix *un–*

A **prefix** is a word part added to the beginning of a **base word**. It changes the meaning of the base word. The **prefix** un– can mean "not" or "opposite of."

> ### Word Bank
>
> unwrap   unsafe   unroll   unclean

▶ Choose a word from the box that best completes each sentence. Write the word on the line. Look up any base words you do not know in the dictionary.

1. The road was _____ to drive on.

2. I will _____ my sleeping bag.

3. Jae wants to _____ the gift.

4. His shoes were _____ from walking in the mud.

Name _____

Words to Know

Knowing how to read these words can make you a better reader and writer.

> **Word Bank**
>
> begin   brother   front   picture
>
> room   someone   Sometimes   young

▶ Write the word from the box that best completes each sentence.

_____

- -

1. This is my _____ , Jake.

_____

- -

2. We sleep in the same _____ .

_____

- -

3. The room is at the _____ of the home.

_____

- -

4. _____ we play together.

_____

- -

5. Jake is _____ I love very much.

Grade 1

Module 10 • Week 1

Name _____

Contractions with *'m*, *'s*, *n't*, *'ll*

A **contraction** is a short form of two words put together. An apostrophe (') takes the place of the letter or letters that are dropped.

I am → **I'm**   it is → **it's**   is not → **isn't**   I will → **I'll**

▶ Write each Spelling Word in the correct box.

Words with *n't*

_____

- - - - - - - - - - -

_____

_____

- - - - - - - - - - -

_____

_____

- - - - - - - - - - -

_____

_____

Words with *'m*

_____

- - - - - - - - - - -

Words with *'ll*

_____

- - - - - - - - - - -

_____

_____

- - - - - - - - - - -

_____

Words with *'s*

_____

- - - - - - - - - - -

_____

_____

- - - - - - - - - - -

_____

Name _____

Contractions with 've, 're

A **contraction** is a short form of two words put together. To make a contraction, an apostrophe (') takes the place of one or more letters. The word **we're** is the contraction for **we are**. The word **you've** is a contraction for **you have**.

▶ Say the words in bold print a shorter way. Then write the contraction to complete each sentence.

1. **You are** _____ the winner.

2. **I have** _____ never read that book.

3. **They have** _____ made the best hot dogs.

4. **We are** _____ helping Dad in the yard.

5. **They are** _____ my pals.

Name _____

Contractions with 'm, 's, n't, 'll

A **contraction** is a short form of two words put together. An apostrophe (') takes the place of the letter or letters that are dropped.

I am → **I'm**   it is → **it's**   is not → **isn't**   I will → **I'll**

▶ Write the Spelling Word that is the contraction of the two words in ( ).

_____

1. (I will) _____ go next week.

_____

2. He (is not) _____ home yet.

_____

3. (We will) _____ sing the new song.

_____

4. (That is) _____ my teacher.

_____

5. She (did not) _____ go to school.

_____

6. (I am) _____ a good ball player.

Spelling Words
Basic
I'm
can't
isn't
we'll
you'll
it's
didn't
that's
I'll
wasn't
Review
cents
catches
long
thank

Name _____

Phonics Review

A **contraction** is a short form of two words put together. An apostrophe (') takes the place of one or more letters. **We're** is the contraction for **we are**. **I've** is the contraction for **I have**.

▶ Combine the words to write each contraction.

1. <u>You are</u> my best pal.   _____

                                                            _____

2. <u>We have</u> been pals a long time.   _____

A **suffix** is a word part added to the end of a word to change its meaning. The **suffix –er** helps us compare two people or things. The **suffix –est** helps us compare more than two people or things.

▶ Add **–er** or **–est** to the word **fast** to complete each sentence.

                                                 _____

1. My bike is fast, but a car is _____ .

                                        _____

2. A plane is the _____ of all three.

Power Words: Match

Word Bank

floor   straight   designed   whole   real   model

▶ Write the Power Word from **Young Frank Architect** that best fits each item.

1. Which word means almost the same as **planned**?

    _____

2. This word describes something that is not bent or curved.

    _____

3. Which word means **not make-believe?**

    _____

4. Which word names something that looks the same as something bigger?

    _____

5. Which word means **all of something?**

    _____

6. Which word names a part of a tall building?

    _____

Name _____

Prefix *re–*

A **prefix** is a word part that changes the meaning of a **base word**. The **prefix re–** can mean "again."

▶ Add the **prefix re–** to each base word in the box. Then write one of the new words to finish each sentence. Use a dictionary to look up any words you do not know.

```
                        Word Bank
  paint            fill            read            plant
```

_____   _____
- - - - - - - - - - - - -   - - - - - - - - - - - - -
_____   _____

_____   _____
- - - - - - - - - - - - -   - - - - - - - - - - - - -
_____   _____

1. Mom will _____ the cup.

2. Dad had to _____ the seeds.

3. I want to _____ this book!

4. Jess will _____ the walls.

Name _____

Setting

The **setting** of a story is where and when it takes place. Readers can use **details** in the words and pictures to **describe** the setting. The setting can be the place, time of day, time of year, or season when the story takes place.

▶ Answer the questions about **Young Frank Architect**.

🔍 Pages 118–120 Where and when does this part of the story take place? What evidence tells you this?

_____

- -

_____

_____

- -

_____

_____

- -

_____

🔍 Pages 126–129 How has the setting changed? What evidence tells you this?

_____

- -

_____

_____

- -

_____

Name _____

Shades of Meaning

Synonyms are words that mean the same or almost the same thing. Small differences in the meanings of words are called **shades of meaning**.

▶ Read each group of synonyms. Then write the words in order from the weakest to the strongest meaning.

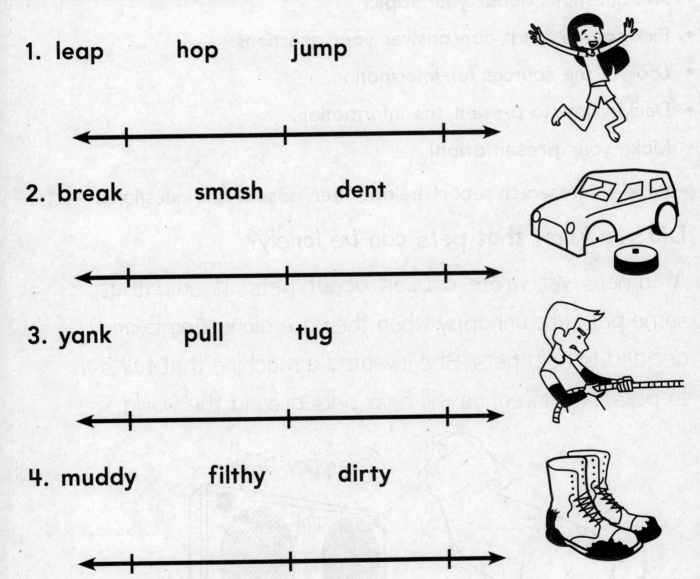

1. leap   hop   jump

2. break   smash   dent

3. yank   pull   tug

4. muddy   filthy   dirty

Name _____

Present Information

When you want to learn more about a topic, you can make a plan to help find the information you want.

Here are some important steps to take:

- Make a plan.

- Ask questions about your **topic**.

- Pick **sources** that can answer your questions.

- Look in the sources for information.

- Decide how to present the information.

- Make your **presentation**!

▶ Read the research report below. Then answer the questions.

Did you know that pets can be lonely?

A famous vet wrote a book about pets. It said that some pets are unhappy when they are alone. Jen Evans decided to help pets. She invented a machine that talks to pets. Her invention will help pets around the world.

Good boy, Spot!

Name _____

1. What is the topic of the research report?

_____

- -

_____

2. What is one source the writer used?

_____

- -

_____

3. What information did the writer get from that source?

_____

- -

_____

4. What other source could the writer have used?

_____

- -

_____

5. How did the writer present the information?

_____

- -

_____

_____

- -

_____

Name _____

Words to Know

▶ Write the word that best completes each sentence.

_____

- - - - - - - - - - - - - - -

1. I _____ to get to the park.

_____

- - - - - - - - - - - - - - -

2. I have _____ here before.

_____

- - - - - - - - - - - - - - -

3. My pals and I play here _____.

_____

- - - - - - - - - - - - - - -

4. We _____ the bugs in the grass.

_____

- - - - - - - - - - - - - - -

5. We _____ a bird sing a song.

_____

- - - - - - - - - - - - - - -

6. I _____ my day at the park.

▶ Write a sentence for a word you did not write yet.

_____

- -

_____

Name _____

Words with oo (/o͝o/)

You can spell the /o͝o/ sound with **oo**, as in **book**.

▶ Write each Spelling Word in the correct box.

Spelling Words

Basic

book

good

hook

brook

took

foot

wool

shook

wood

boyhood

Review

isn't

we'll

that's

you'll

Words with *ook*

_____

- - - - - - - - - - - - - - -

_____

- - - - - - - - - - - - - - -

_____

- - - - - - - - - - - - - - -

_____

- - - - - - - - - - - - - - -

_____

- - - - - - - - - - - - - - -

_____

Words with *ood*

_____

- - - - - - - - - - - - - - -

_____

- - - - - - - - - - - - - - -

_____

- - - - - - - - - - - - - - -

_____

- - - - - - - - - - - - - - -

_____

Words with *oot*

_____

- - - - - - - - - - - - - - -

_____

Words with *ool*

_____

- - - - - - - - - - - - - - -

_____

Name _____

Words with *oo* (/o͝o/)

The vowel team **oo** can stand for the vowel sound in **look**.

▶ Write the correct word to complete each sentence.

1. I want to read this _____ .

   brook　　　**boat**　　　**book**

2. I put up my _____ when it rains.

   hood　　　**hook**　　　**hard**

3. The _____ will make lunch.

   cool　　　**kick**　　　**cook**

4. I bumped my _____ on the rock.

   woof　　　**foot**　　　**soot**

5. Mom _____ the train to work.

   told　　　**stood**　　　**took**

Name _____

Words with *oo* (/o͝o/)

You can spell the /o͝o/ sound with **oo**, as in **took**.

▶ Write the Basic Spelling Word that names each picture.

Spelling Words

Basic

book
good
hook
brook
took
foot
wool
shook
wood
boyhood

Review

isn't
we'll
that's
you'll

1.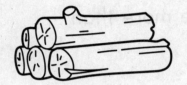

_____

- - - - - - - - - - - -

_____

2.

_____

- - - - - - - - - - - -

_____

3.

_____

- - - - - - - - - - - -

_____

4.

_____

- - - - - - - - - - - -

_____

5.

_____

- - - - - - - - - - - -

_____

6.

_____

- - - - - - - - - - - -

_____

Power Words: Draw and Write

Word Bank

artist   gallery   mural   rummaged

▶ Draw a picture or write words that will help you remember each Power Word from **Sky Color**. Try to write more than you draw.

1. artist	**2. gallery**
3. mural	**4. rummaged**

Name _____

Theme

The **topic** is what a story is mostly about. The **theme** is the big idea about the topic. Readers can identify the theme by looking for the lesson, or **moral**, the author wants readers to take away from the story. Look for the lesson that a character learns or teaches to help you figure out a story's theme.

▶ Answer the questions about **Sky Color.**

🔍 Pages 142–144 Why is Marisol having a difficult time?

_____

- -

_____

- -

_____

🔍 Pages 150–152 What did Marisol learn? What does the author want you to learn from reading this story?

_____

- -

_____

- -

_____

- -

_____

Name _____

Phonics Review

The vowel team **oo** can stand for the vowel sound in **look**.

When a word ends in a **consonant + le** syllable, divide the word before the consonant. Examples: **puzzle = puz / zle**, **tumble = tum / ble**.

▶ Write two words to complete each sentence.

_____   _____

1. A _____ swims in the _____ .

   brook   book   turtle   tunnel

_____   _____

2. Dad has a _____ of _____ .

   bowl   fables   fumbles   book

_____   _____

3. I _____ happy when I _____ .

   like   giggle   goggle   look

_____   _____

4. The _____ bakes an _____ pie.

   coat   attic   apple   cook

Name _____

Words About Places and Things

Nouns are words that name a person, a place, or a thing.

- A noun that names a place tells **where** something is.

- A noun that names a thing tells **what** something is.

▶ Read each noun. Write **P** if it names a **place**. Write **T** if it names a **thing**. Use a dictionary to find the meanings of any words you don't know.

1. fence _____

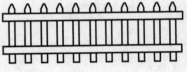

2. ball _____

3. backyard _____

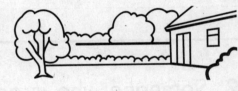

4. lake _____

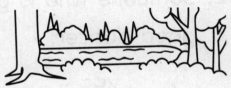

▶ Choose a noun that names a **thing** and a noun that names a **place** to finish this sentence.

5. We played _____ near the _____ .

Grade 1

283

Module 10 • Week 2

Power Words: Yes or No?

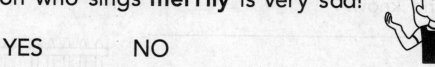

Word Bank

merrily   promise

▶ Read each sentence. Circle **YES** if the word makes sense or **NO** if it does not. Rewrite the sentence so it makes sense.

1. A person who sings **merrily** is very sad!

YES   NO

- -

- -

2. Someone who is good at drawing shows **promise** to be a good dancer.

YES   NO

- -

- -

Name _____

Elements of Poetry

Poets have special ways to make their poems fun to read. **Alliteration** is when words start with the same sound or sounds. **Repetition** is when the same words or lines are said over and over. **Rhyme** happens when words end with the same sound or sounds. When sounds or words are repeated, they make a **pattern**.

▶ Answer the questions about **We Are the Future.**

🔍 Page 162 Why does the author repeat the words **times two**? What else do you notice about these words?

_____

_____

_____

_____

_____

_____

🔍 Pages 166–167 How do the poets use words and sounds to make the poems fun to read?

_____

_____

_____

Name _____

Words to Know

> ### Word Bank
>
> bear   color   happy   money
>
> music   second   sound   without

▶ Circle the word that best completes each sentence.

1. Mom gave Bill a toy (second, bear).

2. The (color, music) of the bear is tan.

3. The gift made Bill feel (money, happy).

4. His (second, happy) gift was a toy boat.

5. Mom likes to play (music, without) for us.

6. We like the (second, sound) of the music.

Name _____

Vowel Patterns: /o͞o/

You can spell the /o͞o/ sound with **oo**, as in **moon**, with **ew**, as in **new**, and with **ou**, as in **soup**.

▶ Write each Spelling Word in the correct column.

Words with *oo*	Words with *ew*	Words with *ou*

Spelling Words

Basic

soon

new

noon

zoo

boot

too

moon

blew

soup

you

Review

book

foot

brook

boyhood

Name _____

Vowel Patterns: /o͞o/

The vowel patterns **oo**, **ou**, and **ew** can all spell the vowel sound you hear in **moose**.

▶ Read the question and look at the picture. Write the word that answers the question.

Is it **soap** or **soup**?

_____
- - - - - - - - - - - - - -
_____

Is it a **stool** or a **stone**?

_____
- - - - - - - - - - - - - -
_____

Is it a **groom** or a **group**?

_____
- - - - - - - - - - - - - -
_____

Can it **scoop** or **scope**?

_____
- - - - - - - - - - - - - -
_____

Is it a **pole** or a **pool**?

_____
- - - - - - - - - - - - - -
_____

Is it a **stew** or a **step**?

_____
- - - - - - - - - - - - - -
_____

Name _____

Vowel Patterns: /o͞o/

You can spell the /o͞o/ sound with **oo**, as in **soon**, with **ew**, as in **blew**, and with **ou**, as in **you**.

▶ Read each clue. Unscramble the word. Write the Spelling Word correctly on the line.

_____

1. Not old   **enw** _____

_____

2. Where animals are   **ooz** _____

_____

3. Goes on your foot   **tboo** _____

_____

4. Also   **oto** _____

_____

5. Not later   **oson** _____

_____

6. Something you eat   **puos** _____

Spelling Words

Basic

soon

new

noon

zoo

boot

too

moon

blew

soup

you

Review

book

foot

brook

boyhood

Power Words: Match

Word Bank

build   scraps   neat   golden   usually

▶ Write the Power Word from **Joaquín's Zoo** that best fits each item.

1. Which word means the opposite of **messy**?

   _____

2. Which word names a color?

   _____

3. Which word means almost the same thing as **make**?

   _____

4. Which word tells about what is left over after someone uses something?

   _____

5. Which word tells about something that happens most of the time?

   _____

Name _____

Characters

A **character** is the person, animal, or thing a story is about. Look for clues in the words and pictures to get to know the characters. Describe what characters look like and what they think, feel, say, and do. Understanding what a character is like can help you understand the **reasons** for their **actions**, or why they do what they do.

▶ Answer the questions about **Joaquín's Zoo.**

🔍 Pages 178–180 Who is the main character? What do you know about him?

_____

- -

_____

🔍 Pages 186–188 Why did Joaquín make the animals? How do you know?

_____

- -

_____

- -

_____

_____

- -

_____

Name _____

Phonics Review

Some vowel sounds have more than one spelling pattern. The vowel patterns **oo, ou, ew, ue,** and **u** can all spell the vowel sound you hear in **moose.** Here are more examples: **you, few, due, flu.**

▶ Choose and write the word that completes each sentence.

_____

1. Mom got a _____ dress.

   now   **new**   **news**

   _____

2. I will stick on the shapes with _____.

   clue   **chew**   **glue**

   _____

3. The boy is sick with the _____.

   flu   **flute**   **fool**

   _____

4. The _____ is bright at night.

   moan   **moon**   **mew**

Name _____

Prefix re–

A **prefix** is a word part that changes the meaning of a
base word. The **prefix re–** can mean "again."

▶ Add the **prefix re–** to the words in the box to make new
words. Then use one of the new words to finish each sentence.
Use a dictionary to look up any words you do not know.

Word Bank

wash	send	count	tie

_____   _____

_____   _____

_____

1. I had to _____ the letter.

2. Alex will _____ the red beads.

3. Dad has to _____ his shoes.

4. Mom can _____ my sweater.

Name _____

Words to Know

Knowing how to read and write these words can make you a better reader and writer.

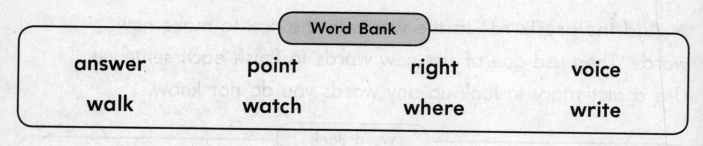

Word Bank

answer	point	right	voice
walk	watch	where	write

▶ Write a word from the box to complete each sentence.

_____

- -

1. Every day, I _____ with my dog Rex.

_____

- -

2. We turn _____ at the bus stop.

_____

- -

3. I use my _____ to tell Rex, "Come!"

_____

- -

4. He will _____ me with a bark.

_____

- -

5. I _____ to a big cat under a tree.

Vowel Diphthongs *ow*, *ou* (/ou/)

You can spell the **/ou/** sound with **ow**, as in **cow**, or **ou**, as in **ouch**.

▶ Write each Basic Spelling Word in the correct column.

Words with
ow

Words with
ou

Basic

how

now

cow

owl

ouch

house

found

out

gown

town

Review

too

boot

new

blew

Name _____

Diphthongs *ow*, *ou*

The words **how** and **out** have the same vowel sound (a diphthong). The special vowel teams **ow** and **ou** spell that sound.

▶ Choose and write the word that names the picture.

clown	crowd		count	cloud	

_____

- - - - - - - - - - -

_____

brown	blouse		found	frown	

_____

- - - - - - - - - - -

_____

coach	couch		mouse	moose	

_____

- - - - - - - - - - -

_____

Name _____

Vowel Diphthongs *ow, ou* (/ou/)

You can spell the **/ou/** sound with **ow**, as in **now**, or **ou**, as in **house**.

▶ Write the missing letters. Then write the Spelling Word on the line.

1. t_____n
   _____   _____

2. c_____
   _____   _____

3. _____t
   _____   _____

4. f_____nd
   _____   _____

5. g_____n
   _____   _____

6. h_____se
   _____

Spelling Words

Basic

how

now

cow

owl

ouch

house

found

out

gown

town

Review

too

boot

new

blew

Name _____

Phonics Review

The words **how** and **out** have the same vowel sound (a diphthong). The special vowel teams **ow** and **ou** spell that sound. The words **toy** and **oil** have another vowel sound. The special vowel teams **oy** and **oi** spell that sound.

▶ Choose and write the word that completes each sentence. You will not use all the words.

Word Bank
loud   joy   found   spoil   frowns   moist

1. The milk will _____ if you leave it out.

2. Matt _____ the toy mouse under the couch.

3. Water the plant to keep the soil _____ .

4. When I play _____ music, my dog howls.

5. That boy _____ when he feels like a grouch.

Name _____

Words to Know

▶ Write the word that best completes each sentence.

_____

_____

1. I _____ to the garden in the park.

2. My mom and I garden

_____

_____

_____ .

3. We _____ all day in the garden.

4. The sun was out, so it was a _____ day.

_____

_____

5. I was happy when we were _____ .

Name _____

Compound Words

A **compound word** is made up of two shorter words.

    see + saw = seesaw

▶ Put the two shorter words together to make a compound word. Write the compound word.

Shorter word	Shorter word	Compound word
rain	coat	
bed	time	
him	self	
sun	set	
in	side	
see	saw	

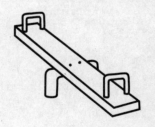

Name _____

Vowel Patterns: /ô/

Sometimes, one vowel sound can have many different spellings. The vowel pattern **aw** spells the vowel sound in the word **saw**. The vowel patterns **au**, **al**, and **all** spell the same sound, as in the words **haul**, **talk**, and **call**.

▶ Choose and write the word that names the picture.

stow straw	auto awning
stalk stall	hawk haul
walk wall	seeing seesaw

Name _____

Compound Words

A **compound word** is made up of two shorter words.

him + self = himself

▶ Write the Spelling Word that names each picture.

Spelling Words

Basic

seesaw

bedtime

sunset

bathtub

sailboat

flagpole

backpack

raincoat

inside

himself

Review

how

ouch

found

gown

1.

_____

_____

2.

_____

_____

3.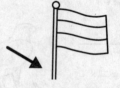

_____

_____

4.

_____

_____

5.

_____

_____

6.

_____

_____

Phonics Review

The vowel patterns **aw**, **au**, **al**, and **all** all spell
the same sound you hear in the word **saw**.

The **–ed** and **–ing** endings help tell when an action
happens. For some words, you must make a spelling
change first:

- Drop the final **e** in a VC*e* word: **hope**, **hoped**, **hoping**.

- Double the final consonant in a CVC short vowel word:
  hop, **hopping**, **hopped**.

▶ Complete each sentence by adding the ending to the
word. Use the spelling rules.

1. sip + ing

_____

Paul is _____ a drink with a straw.

2. crawl + ed

_____

The baby _____ before it walked.

3. tape + ed

_____

Dawn _____ her drawing to the wall.

Name _____

Words to Know

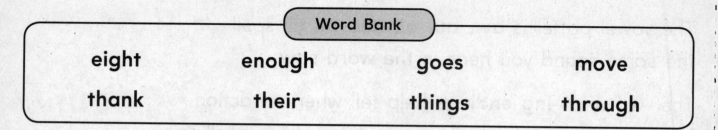

Word Bank
eight · · · · enough · · · · goes · · · · move
thank · · · · their · · · · things · · · · through

▶ Circle the word that best completes each sentence.

1. My family will (thank, move) to a new town.

2. Our new house has (eight, through) rooms.

3. It will be big (their, enough) for all of us.

4. I put the (things, goes) from my room in a box.

5. I walk (through, move) the old house one more time.

6. My brother Sam (their, goes) with me.

Name _____

Inflections –ed, –ing

You can show an action happened in the past by adding **–ed** to some verbs. You can show an action is happening now by adding **–ing** to some verbs.

stay + ed = stayed   stay + ing = staying

▶ Write each Basic Spelling Word in the correct column.

Words with –ed	Words with –ing
_____	_____
_____	_____
_____	_____
_____	_____
_____	_____
_____	_____
_____	_____
_____	_____

Spelling Words
Basic
jumped
stayed
mailed
showed
wishing
needed
flying
staying
seeing
keeping
Review
bedtime
bathtub
sailboat
himself

Name _____

Phonics

Inflections

The **–ed** and **–ing endings** help tell when an action happens.
For some words, you have to make a spelling change first:

- Drop the final **e** in a VC*e* word: **hope, hoped, hoping**.
- Double the final consonant in a CVC short vowel word:
  hop, hopping, hopped.
- Change the final **y** to **i** in a word to add **–ed** but not to
  add **–ing**: **study, studied, studying**.

▶ Add **–ed** and then **–ing** to each word. Use the spelling rules.

	–ed	**–ing**
1. hike	_____	_____
2. copy	_____	_____
3. tap	_____	_____
4. talk	_____	_____
5. jog	_____	_____

Grade 1

© Houghton Mifflin Harcourt Publishing Company. All rights reserved.

306

Module 11 • Week 3

Name _____

Inflections *–ed*, *–ing*

You can show an action happened in the past by adding **–ed** to some verbs. You can show an action is happening now by adding **–ing** to some verbs.

show + ed = showed   fly + ing = flying

▶ Read each sentence. Cross out the Spelling Word that is spelled incorrectly. Write it correctly on the line.

1. He is seing a doctor.
   _____

2. Jim mailled the letter.
   _____

3. The frog jumpd up.
   _____

4. She is keepin him safe.
   _____

5. I stayd home Monday.
   _____

6. The bird is flyin away.
   _____

Phonics Review

- Remember these spelling rules before you add **–ed** or **–ing**: drop the final **e** in VCe words, double the final consonant in CVC words, and change **y** to **i** and add **–ed** in words that end with **consonant + y**.

- There are many ways to spell long **e**. Some less common ways include **ie** as in **chief**, **y** as in **copy**, and **ey** as in **key**.

▶ Choose and write the words that complete each sentence.

1. The _____ team _____ on the ice.

   hockey   **skipping**   **happen**   **skated**

2. The _____ is _____ in the yard.

   hoping   **hopping**   **bunny**   **buggy**

3. The fire _____ _____ the hose.

   cared   **carried**   **chief**   **chef**

4. Mom _____ the pie into six _____ .

   paces   **sliced**   **slicked**   **pieces**

Name _____

Words to Know

Knowing how to read and write these words can make you a better reader and writer.

```
( Word Bank )
    above        again        around       Does
    gives        live         says         What
```

▶ Write a word from the box to complete each sentence.

_____

- - - - - - - - - - - - - - - - -

1. _____ is in the box on the top shelf?

_____

- - - - - - - - - - - - - - - -

2. It is high _____ my head.

_____

- - - - - - - - - - - - - -

3. Mom _____ the box to me.

"_____

- - - - - - - - - - - - - - - -

4. _____ it have your old toys

in it?" she asks.

_____

- - - - - - - - - - - - - - - -

5. I tell her, "Yes! It's fun to see them _____ ."

Name _____

Spelling

Suffixes –*ful*, –*ly*, –*y*

You can add a **suffix**, or ending, to a **base word** to change the word's meaning. Some suffixes are –**ful**, –**ly**, and –**y**.

warm + ly = warmly   help + ful = helpful

▶ Write each Basic Spelling Word in the correct column.

Spelling Words

Basic

warm
warmly
dust
dusty
trick
tricky
help
helpful
hope
hopeful

Review

wishing
mailed
staying
jumped

Base words	Words with suffixes

Grade 1

© Houghton Mifflin Harcourt Publishing Company. All rights reserved.

310

Module 12 • Week 1

Name _____

Suffixes –*ful*, –*less*, –*ly*, –*y*

A **suffix** is a syllable, or word part, added to the end of a word to change its meaning. The **suffix –ful** means "full of," as in **helpful**. The **suffix –less** means "without," as in **careless**. The **suffix –ly** means "in that way," as in **loudly**. The **suffix –y** means "like," as in **snowy**.

▶ Choose and write a word to complete each sentence.

_____

- - - - - - - - - - - - - - - - - -

1. The car drives _____ down the street.

   quickly   **quitting**   **quacked**

_____

- - - - - - - - - - - - - - - - - -

2. I like to fly a kite on a _____ day.

   wildly   **windless**   **windy**

_____

- - - - - - - - - - - - - - - - - -

3. If you do not lie, you are _____ .

   toothless   **truthful**   **thanking**

_____

- - - - - - - - - - - - - - - - - -

4. He is so brave that he is _____ .

   fearful   **fearless**   **fearing**

Name _____

Suffixes –ful, –ly, –y

You can add a **suffix**, or ending, to a **base word** to change the word's meaning. Some suffixes are –ful, –ly, and –y.

trick + y = tricky   hope + ful = hopeful

▶ Read each clue. Unscramble the word. Write the Spelling Word correctly on the line.

1. Hard   **ykctri**   _____

2. Full of hope   **pelufho**   _____

3. Tiny bits of
   dirt   **sudt**   _____

4. Not cool   **mwra**   _____

5. Not clean   **yutsd**   _____

6. Giving help   **lplufhe**   _____

Spelling Words

Basic

warm
warmly
dust
dusty
trick
tricky
help
helpful
hope
hopeful

Review

wishing
mailed
staying
jumped

Name _____

Phonics Review

A **suffix** is a syllable added to the end of a word to change its meaning. The **suffix –ful** means "full of." The **suffix –less** means "without." The **suffix –ly** means "in that way." The **suffix –y** means "like."

A **prefix** is a syllable added to the beginning of a word to change its meaning. The **prefix re–** means "again." The **prefix un–** means "not" or "opposite."

▶ Choose and write the word that completes each sentence. You will not use all the words.

> **Word Bank**
>
> rewrite   endless   rocky   useful   unplug   safely

1. Look both ways to cross the street _____.

2. I can _____ my paper to make it neater.

3. Mom will _____ the clogged sink.

4. A step stool is _____ for reaching high places.

313

Name _____

Words to Know

▶ Write the word that best completes each sentence.

_____

----

1. _____ needs a car wash?

_____

----

2. _____ cars have a lot of

dirt on them.

_____

----

3. The _____ who work here

will wash the cars.

_____

----

4. _____ bring soap and water.

_____

----

5. They use _____ to get rid of the

soap suds.

_____

----

6. _____ the cars look clean,

they dry them with soft cloths.

Name _____

Prefixes *re–*, *un–*

You can add a **prefix**, or word part, to the beginning of a **base word** to change the word's meaning. Some prefixes are **re–** and **un–**.

re + shape = reshape   un + tie = untie

▶ Write each Basic Spelling Word in the correct column.

Words with *re–*	Words with *un–*
_____	_____
_____	_____
_____	_____
_____	_____
_____	_____
_____	_____
_____	_____

Spelling Words

Basic

reshape
retry
untie
unhappy
redo
recount
replay
unpack
unhelpful
unkind

Review

helpful
warmly
dusty
tricky

Name _____

Two-Syllable Words: CV, CVC

An **open syllable** has a CV pattern. It ends with one vowel and has a long vowel sound. A **closed syllable** has a CVC pattern. It is closed by one or more consonants and has a short vowel sound. You can use what you know about open and closed syllables to read longer words.

The word **remix** has two syllables, **re-mix**. It has one open syllable, **re**, and one closed syllable, **mix**.

▶ Choose and write the word that names the picture.

1. **basket**   **baby**   **bath**

_____

- -

_____

2. **rabbit**   **roasted**   **robot**

_____

- -

_____

3. **mason**   **muse**   **music**

_____

- -

_____

4. **penny**   **pony**   **pointy**

_____

- -

_____

Name _____

Prefixes *re–*, *un–*

You can add a **prefix**, or word part, to the beginning of a **base word** to change the word's meaning. Some prefixes are **re–** and **un–**.

re + play = replay   un + kind = unkind

▶ Write the missing letters. Then write the Spelling Word on the line.

1. _____kind   _____

2. _____try   _____

3. _____count   _____

4. _____helpful   _____

5. _____happy   _____

6. _____play   _____

Spelling Words

Basic

reshape
retry
untie
unhappy
redo
recount
replay
unpack
unhelpful
unkind

Review

helpful
warmly
dusty
tricky

Name _____

Phonics Review

An **open syllable** has a CV pattern. It ends in one vowel and has a long vowel sound. A **closed syllable** has a CVC pattern. It is closed by one or more consonants and has a short vowel sound. Use what you know about open and closed syllables to read longer words. Example: The word **pupil** has two syllables, **pu-pil**. It has one open syllable, **pu**, and one closed syllable, **pil**.

▶ Choose and write a word to complete each sentence.

1. The _____ spun a big web.

   spider   **spying**   **speedy**

2. Emma will _____ to your letter soon.

   replay   **rely**   **reply**

3. We will sleep in a _____ on our trip.

   holly   **hotter**   **hotel**

4. I rode a _____ at the farm.

   pony   **phone**   **party**

Name _____

Words to Know

Word Bank

animal	could	different	pull
should	talk	won't	would

▶ Circle the word that best completes each sentence.

1. I (would, pull) like to get a pet.

2. Which kind of (animal, talk) should I get?

3. (Should, Pull) I get a pony?

4. Maybe a (could, different) animal would be better.

5. Maybe I (talk, could) get a rabbit.

6. A rabbit (won't, animal) need as much room.

Name _____

Suffixes *–er*, *–est*

You can add the **suffix –er** to a **base word** to compare two things. You can add the **suffix –est** to a base word to compare more than two things.

hard + er = harder   hard + est = hardest

▶ Write each Basic Spelling Word in the correct column.

Base words	Words with *–er*	Words with *–est*
_____	_____	_____
_____	_____	_____
_____	_____	_____
_____	_____	_____
_____	_____	_____
_____	_____	_____
_____	_____	_____

Spelling Words

Basic

hard

harder

hardest

fast

faster

fastest

slower

slowest

sadder

saddest

Review

replay

unhappy

unkind

redo

Name _____

Suffixes –er, –est

A **suffix** is a syllable added to the end of a **base word** to change its meaning. Use the **suffix –er** to compare two people or things. Use the **suffix –est** to compare more than two people or things: **fast**, **faster**, **fastest**.

If a word has a short vowel CVC pattern, double the final consonant before adding **–er** or **–est**: **sad**, **sadder**, **saddest**.

▶ Choose and write a word to complete each sentence.

```
┌─────────────────── Word Bank ───────────────────┐
│  hottest    dimmer    colder    reddest    taller  │
└──────────────────────────────────────────────────┘
```

1. Tim picked the _____ apple on the tree.

2. Summer is the _____ time of year.

3. Val is an inch _____ than I am.

4. I put ice in the drink to make it _____ .

5. A weak light is _____ than a strong lamp.

Name _____

Suffixes –er, –est

You can add the **suffix –er** to a **base word** to compare two things. You can add the **suffix –est** to a base word to compare more than two things.

fast + er = faster   fast + est = fastest

▶ Read each word. Follow the directions. Write the Spelling Word on the line.

Basic

hard

harder

hardest

fast

faster

fastest

slower

slowest

sadder

saddest

Review

replay

unhappy

unkind

redo

1. slowest	Change **est** to **er**.
2. hard	Add **er**.
3. fast	Add **est**.
4. harder	Change **er** to **est**.
5. fastest	Take away **est**.
6. saddest	Change **est** to **er**.

Phonics Review

Sometimes you need to make spelling changes to add the **suffixes –er** and **–est** or the **endings –ed, –ing, –s,** or **–es** to a **base word**.

For a VC*e* word, drop the final **e: smile, smiled, smiling.**

For a CVC word, double the final consonant: **hop, hopped, hopping.**

For a word with final consonant **y,** change **y** to **i: study, studies, studied.**

▶ Do the word problems. Use the spelling rules to help you.

Add **ing** to **save.**

_____

- - - - - - - - - - - - - - -

_____

Add **ed** to **hope.**

_____

- - - - - - - - - - - - - - -

_____

Add **es** to **pony.**

_____

- - - - - - - - - - - - - - -

_____

Add **ing** to **tap.**

_____

- - - - - - - - - - - - - - -

_____

Add **er** to **wet.**

_____

- - - - - - - - - - - - - - -

_____

Add **ed** to **hurry.**

_____

- - - - - - - - - - - - - - -

_____